Investing in the Trump Era

Nicholas P. Sargen

Investing in the Trump Era

How Economic Policies Impact Financial Markets

Nicholas P. Sargen
Fort Washington Investment Advisors
Cincinnati, OH, USA

ISBN 978-3-319-76044-5   ISBN 978-3-319-76045-2   (eBook)
https://doi.org/10.1007/978-3-319-76045-2

Library of Congress Control Number: 2018936511

Cover design: Getty Images / illixr

Printed on acid-free paper

This Palgrave Macmillan imprint is published by the registered company Springer International Publishing AG part of Springer Nature.
The registered company address is: Gewerbestrasse 11, 6330 Cham, Switzerland

PREFACE

The 2016 presidential election campaign was unlike any in our lifetimes. It pitted a well-known political figure, Hillary Clinton, against a real estate mogul and television celebrity, Donald Trump, with no political background or apparent ideology. The televised debates, while lively at times, disintegrated into a morass. Instead of being enlightened about public policy issues, many Americans were frustrated and bewildered with the process, the politicians and the media alike.

Unfortunately, the situation worsened following the election. President Trump accused the media of creating "fake news," and the gulf between Republicans and Democrats in Congress reached the point where passage of bipartisan legislation is all but impossible. Amid this polarization, people are left to their own devices to understand public policy issues, and most wind up listening or reading sources that share their political orientation and which reinforce their views.

The reality is the most controversial issues are also the most complex. They entail considering trade-offs and making value judgments. If they were easy to fix, they would not be a long-standing problem. Moreover, some issues that are highly political—such as repeal and replacement of Obamacare—have only limited impact on financial markets. The reason: The legislation impacts only a small segment of the healthcare sector.

Amid this backdrop, my primary goal in writing this book is to provide an objective source for investors and the public to learn about economic policy issues that surfaced in the 2016 election but which have evolved over time. Topics covered relate to long-term economic growth, the federal budget deficit, healthcare reform, tax reform, regulatory policies affecting the environment and financial system, the nexus of monetary, exchange rate and trade policies, and globalization and its effects on income distribution.

The book tackles each of these issues systematically. First, it provides context to understand how the respective issue evolved over time, and it then discusses the current context. Second, the book presents evidence on each issue that is based on studies by experts in the respective fields. Third, it presents views from both sides of the political divide, so the reader can form his or her own opinion. Finally, the results are distilled in the final chapter, in which I offer my personal conclusions on the recommended policies.

A related goal of the book is to assess what the likely impact of the respective policies will be on financial markets. While the 2016 presidential election was close, the markets' response was decisive: The United States and global equity markets went on a tear as consumer and business confidence soared. This surprised many investors who believed a Trump victory would be bad for financial markets. It also caused many to question whether expectations embedded in markets were too optimistic. My assessment of how financial markets are likely to play out is presented in the opening and concluding chapters.

ORGANIZATION

The book contains ten chapters that are organized into four sections: (i) Financial Markets and Long-Term Growth; (ii) Fiscal and Regulatory Policies to Promote Growth; (iii) Monetary, Exchange Rate and Trade Policies; and (iv) Globalization and Financial Markets. They serve as building blocks so the reader can grasp how various issues are interrelated rather than simply viewing each of them in isolation.

Section I. Financial Markets and Long-Term Growth

The first section focuses on the way financial markets respond to the prospects for improved long-term growth and whether policies under consideration can achieve this objective.

Chapter 1. Is Trump's Election a Game-Changer?

The opening chapter serves as an overview for the book and presents my assessment of the state of the US economy and financial markets at the beginning of 2017. Investors at the time were trying to fathom where President Trump would take the country. My message was to treat tweets and off-the-cuff statements as noise and to focus instead on the policies that are enacted, as they are what will impact the economy and markets. One challenge was that little was known then about legislation the Trump administration and Republican leadership in Congress would propose. Consequently, my advice for investors was to be flexible and modify their assessments as the legislative process unfolded.

The prospective policies are grouped into three buckets: "Good for markets" (tax reform and deregulation); "Bad for markets" (outsized budget and trade deficits) and "Ugly" (risk of protectionism). My assessment was the US economy would experience somewhat faster growth in the near term because of an improvement in the global economy, but there were formidable challenges to restoring long-term growth. The ability of the stock market to continue its upward trend hinged, in part, on which set of policies would be enacted and whether they can achieve their stated objectives. While the stock market was likely to respond positively to the prospect of corporate tax cuts, the best outcome for the economy entailed undertaking reforms to the tax code, entitlement programs and regulatory structure that would lay the foundation for long-term growth.

Chapter 2. Challenges to Restoring Long-Term Economic Growth
The second chapter examines whether the Trump Administration's policies can restore real GDP growth to its pre-financial crisis trend of 3% per annum. This is a critical element of the President's goal to "Make America Great Again." To do so, labor productivity would have to grow considerably faster than the subpar pace of the past decade and labor force participation rates would have to rise again. However, most economists are skeptical.

The chapter presents several competing explanations for the growth slowdown including (i) a post-financial crisis hangover, (ii) "secular stagnation", (iii) structural impediments to improved productivity and (iv) government interference that impedes market forces and which adds to uncertainty. It then considers the respective policy recommendations of each view. The most optimistic scenario is the latter one, as it presumes a combination of tax reform, deregulation and pro-business policies can boost long-term growth. While it will take years before we know whether productivity is improving, an early indicator is whether business capital spending accelerates.

Section II. Fiscal and Regulatory Policies to Promote Growth

This section delves deeper into the role that fiscal and regulatory policies may play in influencing trend growth, the federal budget deficit and interest rates. Chapters 3, 4 and 5 discuss prospects for the federal budget deficit, healthcare reform and tax reform (corporate and personal), while Chap. 6 features the impact of regulatory changes on two key areas—the environment and the financial system.

Chapter 3. Assessing the US Fiscal Imbalance: Why It Matters
The central message of Chap. 3 is the federal government faces a serious fiscal challenge that can no longer be ignored because of the growing number of baby boomers who are retiring and the aging of the population. Analysis by the Congressional Budget Office (CBO) suggests that absent any policy changes, expenses for mandated programs—Social Security, Medicare and Medicaid—will absorb all federal revenues a decade from now. If entitlement spending is not curbed (and taxes are not raised), the only way to contain the budget deficit is by shrinking other discretionary items. This prospect became apparent when the director of Office of Management and Budget (OMB) unveiled the administration's plan calling for a 9% increase in military and security spending and steep cutbacks in social programs, which spawned a wave of protests.

The chapter also considers the risks entailed in not doing anything. While a full-blown crisis in confidence is unlikely, the combination of the Federal Reserve gradually shrinking its holdings of treasuries while budget imbalances balloon raises the specter of market instability. At some point, interest rates could spike, which would exacerbate the federal government's funding problem and eventually unsettle the stock market.

Chapter 4. What Makes Healthcare Reform So Complex: A Primer
The fourth chapter delves into health care, the fastest growing segment of the federal budget and one of the most contentious issues in the election. The desire to expand insurance coverage while also containing the surge in medical costs in recent decades was the principal objective of the Affordable Care Act (ACA). Today, even supporters of Obamacare concede it has fallen short of its goals, although Democrats maintain the problems can be fixed. For their part, Republicans have been unable to agree on legislation to replace it, despite their philosophical objections.

This begs the question: What makes healthcare reform so difficult, and why have past efforts to rein in costs such as managed care, universal coverage and Obamacare fallen short? The chapter traces the evolution of the US healthcare system in the post-war era and points to a myriad of factors that have undermined previous attempts at reform. One of the principal findings is failure to achieve reform is not simply due to political differences between Republicans and Democrats. Indeed, there are also significant differences among competing power centers—notably, physicians, hospitals, insurers, pharmaceutical companies and employers—that impede reform. In this respect, tackling health care is much more difficult than putting social security on sound footing by extending the age at which recipients receive full benefits.

Chapter 5. Tax Policy: Tax Cuts Versus Tax Reform
The fifth chapter examines the prospect for tax cuts and tax reform. Although the two concepts are often discussed interchangeably, they in fact are very different. President Trump favors steep tax cuts, personal and corporate, to boost the economy, and he has asserted they can be financed via stronger economic growth. By comparison, tax reform has been the hallmark of Speaker Paul Ryan, who is striving to expand the tax base and streamline the tax code by eliminating deductions so the budget deficit does not blow out.

Following the election, investors focused on the House tax bill that was drafted in the summer of 2016. It contained four key elements, of which the most controversial was a border-adjustment tax (BAT) that effectively subsidizes exports while taxing imports. In the wake of the healthcare fiasco, the BAT was dropped, which is estimated to result in a loss of revenues of more than $1 trillion over the next ten years. The bill that was drafted by Congressional Republicans in early November was a mix of tax cuts and tax reform, in which the budget deficit over the coming decade is targeted to increase by $1 trillion. My take is that this outcome is less desirable than the tax reform in the original House Republican bill, but it was necessary to gain passage of tax legislation.

Otherwise, failure to do so would leave Republicans vulnerable in future elections, and it would also result in a stock market sell-off.

Chapter 6. Macroeconomic Effects of Deregulation
Apart from tax incentives, another way to revitalize the economy is via diminished government regulations, which is the subject of Chap. 6. Many businesses have complained about increased regulations during the Obama Administration, and both President Trump and Republicans in Congress strongly endorse lessening regulatory burdens. At the same time, it is difficult for economists to gauge the consequences of regulatory relief for the economy as a whole, and most empirical research has focused on specific industries and a narrow set of regulations.

Recognizing this inherent limitation, the chapter focuses on two of the most controversial areas—namely, regulations affecting the environment and financial services. In the environmental sphere one approach that merits consideration is to find market-oriented solutions to reduce pollutants. This approach has been effective in dealing with the problem of acid rain, but President Trump has been opposed to adopt them to deal with climate control. In the financial arena the case for increased regulation is that financial instability contributed to the severity of the 2008 Global Financial Crisis (GFC). That said, there was also a rush to judgment to pass the Dodd-Frank Act, which many financial institutions contend resulted in regulatory overkill. The challenge policymakers face is to balance the need for increased capital and liquidity requirements without turning financial institutions into regulated utilities.

Section III. Monetary, Exchange Rate and Trade Policies

One issue that influenced the 2016 election was the alleged impact international trade agreements have had on US jobs in manufacturing. For people to grasp this issue fully, they need to understand how international capital flows have become the key driver of trade imbalances since the Reagan years. The chain of causality is that monetary policies influence interest rates and exchange rates, which drive capital flows that affect trade flows.

Chapter 7. Changes in US Monetary Policy: Past and Prospective
Chapter 7 focuses on past and prospective changes in US monetary policy and their impact on the economy and financial markets. While the Federal Reserve is an independent institution, President Trump has the ability to influence it through the appointment of a new chairman and four new governors. The Fed's greatest achievement since the early 1980s, when Paul Volcker served as Fed chair and was succeeded by Alan Greenspan, has been its success in reining in inflation and inflation expectations: It set the stage for strong economic performance and a powerful rally in financial markets that lasted until 1999. Nonetheless, despite this achievement, the Fed has struggled to assure financial stability, and it had to undertake extraordinary actions during and after the GFC to bolster the financial system and foster economic recovery.

The second part of the chapter examines the Fed's pursuit of unorthodox policies called Quantitative Easing (QE), whereby it significantly expanded its balance sheet to combat deflationary pressures. The chapter examines the extent to which these policies have bolstered the economy and lowered the unemployment rate, while also creating significant distortions in capital market prices. The ultimate test of the program's success is how successful the Fed will be in normalizing interest rates and shrinking its balance sheet. While the initial round has gone smoothly, there is considerable uncertainty about how the process will play out in coming years. Meanwhile, investors will be assessing what changes, if any, Jerome Powell and a new leadership team will make to the conduct of monetary policy, particularly when financial markets sell off and/or the economy falters.

Chapter 8. Trade Imbalances and Jobs: A Macro Perspective

Chapter 8 considers President Trump's stance on international trade issues, which was the biggest concern of investors when he was elected. While the Republican Party traditionally has embraced free trade, Trump criticized negotiations over NAFTA and China's entry into the WTO during the campaign, and he threatened to impose across-the-board duties on goods shipped to the United States from China, Mexico and other countries. He also claimed that one of his first actions as President would be to declare China a currency manipulator, although he has since backed off this threat.

This chapter begins by considering the factors that contributed to a ballooning of the US current account deficit since the early 1980s. It next examines the extent to which declines in the US manufacturing jobs can be linked to the US trade imbalances. We find there is no connection between US job losses and NAFTA's creation in the early 1990, and that most of the job declines occurred in the following decade, when China and other Asian economies kept their exchange rates artificially low by acquiring massive quantities of dollar-denominated assets.

The chapter concludes by considering policies to narrow global payments imbalances. Our assessment is the Trump administration's approach to negotiate bilateral trade agreements will likely prove ineffective, and protectionist measures would invite retaliation. An alternative approach would be to have the US government announce it is prepared to purchase assets of countries that are deemed to be currency manipulators. Such an approach would lessen the risk of retaliation and protectionism.

Section IV. Globalization and Financial Markets

The fourth section of the book brings together several issues into a broader context: Namely, have the forces of globalization been positive or negative for the United States and other countries, and what are the prospects for financial markets in coming years?

Chapter 9. Globalization and Widening Income Inequality
The issue of globalization was not formally debated in the US presidential election, but it loomed in the background, as a wave of populism and nationalism spread around the world. Chapter 9 explores why this is happening. Previously, free trade and capital mobility had been viewed favorably, as a means of fostering wealth creation in both advanced economies and emerging economies. The backlash to globalization began in the last decade when countries that were suppliers of raw materials began to compete with industrial economies, and growing numbers of people in advanced countries were displaced or saw their incomes stagnate. In the process, income disparities in the United States increased, and there is a growing division between "The Haves" and "The Have Nots."

This chapter argues that globalization is not the only source of disruption: It has been accompanied by rapid technological change, and many people lack the skills and training to adapt. It explores policy options to address this issue and concludes that improving the quality of education and training for people is essential. One lesson from history is that countries that adapt to changing conditions are the ones that have fared the best, whereas those that do not adapt get left behind. The bottom line is that globalization is not going away, and the strongest countries are the ones that embrace it.

Chapter 10. Economic and Market Prospects for the Medium Term
The final chapter summarizes the main findings of the book and assesses the prospects for the US economy and financial markets over the next few years. On balance, we believe the near-term cyclical conditions are favorable, because the global economy is experiencing a synchronized expansion for the first time since 2010. This suggests that after a decade of adjustment, the fallout from the GFC is fading, and central banks are now in position to begin normalizing monetary policy, with the Federal Reserve leading the way.

However, with the US economy on a steady trajectory and the unemployment rate down to 4%, this is not the time for fiscal stimulus, whether on the spending or tax side of the equation. Instead, this is a good time to undertake reforms that will strengthen the economy over the long term, as baby boomers are retiring and living longer. The policy measures that should be pursued include altering the corporate tax code to make it competitive internationally, reforming entitlement programs to make them actuarially sound and streamlining regulations that hamper smaller businesses and that effectively treat financial institutions as regulated utilities. It is also appropriate to implement policies that will lessen currency manipulation by foreign countries. However, it would be a mistake to revoke NAFTA, and protectionist measures that adversely impact trade would harm the global economy and financial markets. In the end, the prospects for the economy and financial markets hinge on which types of policies are enacted.

Finally, investors must weigh the risks that key legislation may not be enacted. One of the biggest surprises in 2017 was the strong showing of risk assets such as equities and high-yield bonds amid record low volatility, despite the failure to enact any meaningful legislation until late December. Part of the reason is that US corporate profits were boosted by stronger growth abroad and a softer US dollar. Equity investors were also enamored by the prospect of tax cuts, and they are less concerned than bondholders by the budgetary consequences. Nonetheless, they are likely to discover there is no "rosy scenario" in which growth will take care of looming budgetary problem. The reality is the nation faces difficult choices ahead with no easy solutions.

Cincinnati, OH, USA   Nicholas P. Sargen

ACKNOWLEDGMENTS

I wish to thank my friends who have influenced my thinking over the years on the issues in this book. I am particularly grateful to three outstanding physicians—Rhonda Cobin, Mark Golub, and Anthony Spinelli—who provided helpful guidance on healthcare issues. I am also indebted to my colleagues at Fort Washington Investment Advisors, Inc., including Dan Carter, Austin Kummer, and Paul Tomich, who provided research support, and to my assistant, Kathy Louden, who was diligent in preparing the manuscript. Finally, I wish to thank the Western & Southern Financial Group for its support, although the views expressed are solely mine.

CONTENTS

LIST OF FIGURES

LIST OF TABLES

PART I

Financial Markets and Long-Term Growth

CHAPTER 1

Is Trump's Election a Game-Changer?

Donald Trump's victory over Hillary Clinton in November 2016 caught most political pundits and market commentators completely off guard, much like the outcome of the Brexit vote in the United Kingdom. Previously, markets had been priced for a Clinton victory and Republican control of Congress, which spelled more policy gridlock. Following Trump's victory and Republicans retaining control of both houses of Congress, investors became hopeful that a decade of government dysfunction might finally be over.

On the eve of the election the consensus among Wall Street commentators was Trump's chances of winning were low—on the order of 30–35%. Moreover, in the event he pulled off a rare upset, it was widely believed financial markets would sell off, because Trump had no prior political experience and was accustomed to make off-the-cuff statements and tweets. Immediately following the announcement of his victory, the US equity markets plummeted. However, they stabilized soon after, and then began to take off once Trump made a conciliatory speech about his opponent.

In ensuing weeks investors were willing to give the President-elect the benefit of the doubt that his pro-growth agenda would reap benefits in the future. Trump campaigned on a theme of making America great again, and his list of policies included a host of measures favorable to US businesses. After the election, he followed up by appointing several prominent business leaders to Cabinet positions and advisory roles.

The US markets responded with a powerful surge in stocks and somewhat higher bond yields that lasted throughout 2017 (Table 1.1). While the consensus among economic forecasters was the economy would continue to expand close to the 2% trend rate during the current expansion, investors were hopeful that the former growth trend of more than 3% per annum would be restored before long. At the same time, Wall Street analysts revised their projections of S&P 500 corporate profits higher: The consensus called for them to expand by 12% in 2017, which is the high end of the range over the past decade.

© The Author(s) 2018
N. P. Sargen, *Investing in the Trump Era*,
https://doi.org/10.1007/978-3-319-76045-2_1

Table 1.1 Financial market returns, pre- and post-2016 elections through 2017

	Pre (Jan 1–Nov 8)	Post (Nov 8, 2016)
S&P500	6.6%	27.9%
Russell 2000	6.5%	30.5%
EAFE ($)	−0.6%	28.4%
MSCI EM ($)	16.3%	31.9%
US Treasury	3.8%	−0.5%
IG credit	7.8%	4.1%
High yield	15.2%	9.4%

Source: S&P, Frank Russell, MSCI, US Treasury, Barclays, ML

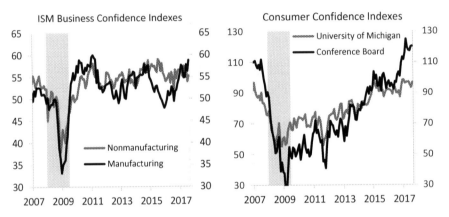

Fig. 1.1 US business and consumer confidence indexes. (Source: ISM, Conference Board, University of Michigan)

Indeed, some commentators observed that Trump's victory unleashed "animal spirits," as confidence readings for both businesses and consumers spiked (see Fig. 1.1). It also spilled over to business surveys for both the manufacturing and services sectors. Within financial markets the term "Trump trade" was used to describe the combination of a surging stock market, rising Treasury yields, narrowing corporate credit spreads and a strong dollar, as well as a general rise in risk assets globally.

Amid these developments many people asked the following question: Will Trump's election mark a turning point for the economy and markets, or are investors' expectations too high? I gave a presentation on that topic just as President Trump assumed office, which helps to frame the issues covered in this book.

ELECTIONS USUALLY HAVE FLEETING IMPACTS ON MARKETS

My answer to the question is that if history is any guide, the market's optimism may prove excessive. The reason: It is rare that presidential elections impact the economy and financial markets for very long. Most of the time the effects are fleeting, and the ultimate outcomes are dictated by factors unrelated to elections.

A notable exception is Ronald Reagan's first election victory.[1] Investors at the time were hopeful President Reagan's "supply-side" policies of tax cuts and regulatory relief and his commitment to low inflation and a strong dollar would transform the American economy, ending a decade of stagflation and pessimism. These hopes were ultimately borne out, but it took several years for Reagan's economic policies to bear fruit.

Even then, credit must be given to Paul Volcker and the Federal Reserve for abandoning policy gradualism in favor of "shock therapy," in which interest rates were allowed to rise to record levels to break the back of inflation and inflation expectations. This resulted in a severe recession and a developing country debt crisis in 1982 that threatened the stability of the world's financial system. However, once the Fed altered course by easing policy aggressively, the stage was set for an ensuing recovery and expansion that proved to be one of the strongest on record. Furthermore, the rally in financial markets that began in mid-1982 continued through Reagan's second term, the administration of George H.W. Bush and throughout the Clinton era, when the United States benefited from a technological renaissance.

The ensuing period from 2000 to 2016 is another story, as both the Bush and Obama Administrations were adversely affected by busts in asset bubbles, first in technology and the second in housing. In both instances, aggressive policy easing by the Federal Reserve helped to contain the fallout to the economy and financial system. However, the trend growth rate of the US economy slowed to about 2% per annum, well below the prior rate of more than 3% in the post-World War II era. This slowdown in economic growth was accompanied by material changes in productivity growth for the economy and in labor force participation rates.

Given this backdrop, the overriding goal of the Trump administration is to restore the glory years before the bursting of the tech and housing bubbles—or what Trump characterized in his campaign motto "Make America Great Again." The challenge facing his administration, therefore, is to formulate a coherent set of policies that not only will revive the economy in the short run, but over the long term as well. In this regard, investors need to have a clear understanding of the ways macroeconomic policies affect economic growth and financial markets so they can formulate a sound investment strategy.

---

[1] In my talk I noted that Margaret Thatcher's election as Britain's Prime Minister in 1979 was another example of a game-changer.

Economic Prospects at the Start of 2017

As President Trump assumed office in January, investors were generally upbeat that the US economy was about to improve and break out of the 2% growth doldrums. Part of the reason is the economy gained traction in the second half of 2016 and the unemployment rate dipped to 4.6%. Personal consumption, which accounts for about 70% of aggregate demand, had been solid, and car sales were running at a record pace.

At the same time, growth abroad was improving, as Europe benefited from persistent low, and even negative, interest rates and a soft euro. The Chinese economy also stabilized in the second half of 2016 from a subpar start, which in turn affected many emerging economies that were suppliers to China. The Japanese economy also showed signs of improvement. Thus, for the first time since 2010, the global economy was on the cusp of a synchronized expansion.

The main factor that excited investors was the prospect of significant changes in policies that would impact the US economy. They included cuts in personal and corporate taxes that were intended to boost consumption and to encourage business capital spending, which had been an area of persistent weakness during the economic expansion. Also, another component of Gross Domestic Product (GDP) that had been unusually weak—government spending—appeared to be set to increase, as the Trump administration was in favor of increased spending for the military. During the campaign, Trump also spoke about the need for a large increase in spending on infrastructure, with the financing to come from a combination of public and private sources. Consequently, it appeared that aggregate demand was poised to accelerate, although the timing and magnitude were uncertain.

In order to achieve *sustained* growth, however, supply-side forces needed to be unleashed as well. The principal reasons some economists are pessimistic about the future are they foresee only modest growth of the labor force and continued low productivity growth. They contend economic growth is likely to remain in the vicinity of 2%—or more than a full percentage point below the post-war average. (This issue is discussed in depth in the Chap. 2.)

The underlying theme of the Trump administration and Congressional Republicans, by comparison, is that subpar growth is mainly a consequence of government policies that have discouraged growth and deterred businesses from investing on plant and equipment. Accordingly, the thrust of their policies is to reinvigorate confidence of business leaders so they are willing to expand business capital spending that is vital to improved productivity growth. Toward this goal, the Trump administration and Republicans in Congress are seeking to reduce and simplify corporate taxes, encourage businesses to repatriate overseas profits and reverse deindustrialization at home, as well as to overhaul the entire regulatory structure.

The chances of getting many of these programs enacted into legislation appeared favorable at the start of 2017, considering the Republicans in Congress shared these goals. However, I noted in the presentation that there were two principal uncertainties investors must weigh: First is the possibility of slippage such that some key legislation does not get enacted; and second, if legislation is enacted, the possibility that it may not produce the desired effects. That said, I did not foresee at the time the problems the President, Paul Ryan and Mitch McConnell would encounter trying to gain support for the repeal and replacement of Obamacare. The wrangling over healthcare also delayed passage of tax reform, which is the cornerstone of the President's agenda. These considerations are discussed in Chaps. 4 and 5.

INVESTORS SHOULD FOCUS ON PENDING LEGISLATION

One of the central messages in my talk was that given the importance of policy changes being considered, investors should focus on pending legislation rather than on the President's predilection for tweets and off-the-cuff statements. While the President's style is certainly unique and may cause an uproar at times, I regard many of his remarks as noise that is likely to have only a limited market impact. By comparison, legislation that is enacted will have a more lasting impact on the economy and markets.

When President Trump assumed office, a key challenge for investors was that legislation had not been drafted in most areas being discussed, and there was only cursory detail about the President's pronouncements. Despite numerous comparisons of "Trump-enomics" and "Reaganomics" (see accompanying box for a comparison), the current situation is very different from the beginning of the Reagan era, when the 1981 Program for Economic Recovery spelled out four major policy objectives. Therefore, since President Trump lacks a coherent political philosophy, I stressed that it was important for investors to monitor developments as they unfolded and to stay flexible.

DISTINGUISHING FEATURES OF REAGANOMICS AND TRUMP-ENOMICS

Pillars of Reaganomics	Core of Trump-enomics
Cut growth of government	Cut discretionary spending ex defense
Lower tax rates for labor and capital	Same
Diminish government regulation	Same
Reduce inflation	No articulation
Commitment to a strong dollar	Favor a weaker dollar
Commitment to free trade	Favor balanced trade

Market participants initially focused on a House Republican tax bill drafted by Speaker Paul Ryan and Republican House leaders in the summer of 2016, because it represented the embodiment of their work on tax reform for many years. The draft bill was intended to be deficit neutral, meaning it attempted to offset losses in revenues from tax cuts by broadening the tax base via reduced deductions and exemptions.

While the House bill applied to both personal and corporate taxes, my contention was that investors would mainly focus on corporate taxes, because they directly affected after-tax corporate profits.[2] The corporate component of the bill contained four key provisions: (i) The corporate tax rate would be lowered from 35% to 20% to make it competitive internationally; (ii) companies could expense all capital outlays immediately but no longer expense interest to remove the current bias favoring debt financing; (iii) companies could repatriate overseas profits at a reduced rate temporarily and (iv) a "border-adjustment tax" (BAT) would be incorporated whereby exports would not count as revenue while imports would not count as costs. Of these provisions, the BAT was deemed the most controversial, because it could risk supply disruptions for retailers and oil refiners, and it may not be permissible under World Trade Organization (WTO) rules.[3] Therefore, the odds that the provision would be included in the final legislation were low.

In the presentation I noted significant differences between the House Republican proposal and the plan that Trump unveiled during the campaign. Specifically, Trump's proposal called for deeper corporate tax cuts and less broadening of the tax base, which meant it was likely to result in a significant expansion of the budget deficit in future years. I noted that the legislation that is ultimately enacted would likely be a compromise between the House Republican plan and the budget proposal the White House would submit via the Office of Management and Budget (OMB).

My take was there were valid reasons for investors to be encouraged that distortions in the existing tax code would be addressed while regulatory burdens would also be reduced significantly. However, the devil is in the details. At the time it was too early to know what legislation would be forthcoming and the associated impacts on the economy and corporate sector. Therefore, I pointed out that investors should not overreact to news stories.

BUDGETARY PRESSURES ARE BUILDING

There are also potential headwinds in the form of enlarged budget deficits in the next few years. Because President Trump is not committed to rein in federal spending, there is considerable risk the budget deficit will balloon. According to the Tax Policy Center, a joint venture of the Urban Institute and the Brookings Institution, Trump's policies would add more than $7 trillion to the budget deficit over the coming decade.[4] It was widely recognized at the time that deficits of this magnitude would be unacceptable to conservative Republicans who worried that the federal debt outstanding was too large.

[2] By comparison, cuts in personal taxes have an indirect effect on corporate profits via increased consumer spending. However, it is difficult to estimate the impact, because important components (such as the income levels to be set for various tax brackets) had not been specified.

[3] See article by Greg Ip., "U.S. Tax Revamp Faces Hurdle in WTO," *Wall Street Journal*, December 22, 2016.

[4] James R. Nunn et al., "Revised Tax Plan," Tax Policy Center, October 18, 2016.

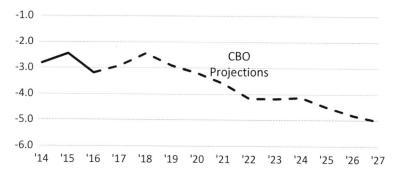

Fig. 1.2 The budget deficit as a % of GDP will deteriorate absent any policy changes. (Source: Congressional Budget Office)

In the absence of any policy changes, the Congressional Budget Office (CBO) projects the federal budget deficit is likely to rise to more than 5% of GDP ten years from now, up from about 2.5% in 2015 (Fig. 1.2).[5] The reason is an aging populace has put added burdens on entitlement programs such as Medicare, Medicaid and Social Security. It was unclear at the time whether Trump would acquiesce to Republican leaders in Congress who believe it is imperative to tackle the entitlements issue head-on. This is discussed in Chap. 3.

A second headwind is the US trade deficit could also expand considerably, which is at odds with the goals of the Trump administration. First, increased government spending on defense and infrastructure will do little to boost exports, while an acceleration in the US growth will pull in imports. Second, US businesses also face the challenge of competing globally in an environment of a strong US dollar, which stood at its highest level on a trade-weighted basis since 2003. Throughout the campaign and as President, Trump repeatedly stated he believed the dollar was too strong, which hurt workers in the manufacturing sector.

This combination of outsized budget and trade imbalances evokes memories of the "twin deficit" problem the United States encountered in the Reagan years. At that time, many investors believed the deficits would generate higher US interest rates. However, they did not materialize, because the Federal Reserve succeeded in reducing inflation and inflation expectations, which ushered in an era of declining interest rates.

Nonetheless, the environment today is diametrically different, with inflation and interest rates near record lows and the Federal Reserve seeking to normalize interest rates. Market participants are expecting bond yields to rise in the next few years, and the specter of the long bond yielding 4% or more in the not-too-distant future is a possibility. If so, it would likely propel the dollar even higher against most currencies.

[5] Congressional Budget Office, "The Budget and Economic Outlook: 2017 to 2027," January 24, 2017.

INTERNATIONAL RISKS

The principal risks that I foresaw at the time were mainly in the international arena, where there was increased potential for conflict with China over its large bilateral trade surplus with the United States, as well as heightened tensions within the European Union (EU) stemming from elections in France, Germany and Italy.

With respect to trade issues, Trump's campaign was filled with rhetoric that China competed unfairly and that multinational trade agreements such as North America Free Trade Agreement (NAFTA) harmed American workers. In his speeches, Trump warned that he would impose duties on imports from China and Mexico to level the playing field. The appointment of Peter Navarro, a professor of economics at the University of California, Irvine, to head the National Trade Council appeared to indicate the Trump administration would be particularly tough on China, as Professor Navarro is an outspoken China critic and the author of *The Coming China Wars.*

It was too early to tell whether the anti-free trade rhetoric was primarily a bargaining ploy, but I maintained it would be a mistake to dismiss it completely. During the campaign, Trump vowed to declare China a currency manipulator and to impose heavy duties on imports from China. However, most of the Chinese currency intervention to lessen the yuan's appreciation occurred before 2015. Since then, China has been trying to limit the RMB's depreciation by selling dollar reserves. If the US government followed through on Trump's campaign threats, the Chinese government could be expected to take strong countermeasures, and financial markets would likely react negatively to the prospect of a looming trade war. As discussed in Chap. 8, the President has since backed away from this stance, as he sought to engage China to rein in North Korea. However, he could alter his position at any time, and investors must be prepared for the fallout.

Another key risk at the start of 2017 was the possibility of added pressures on the EU and the euro. Markets were able to shrug off the results of the British referendum to exit the EU in mid-2016, as well as the rejection of constitutional reforms in Italy that led to the ouster of Matteo Renzi as Italy's Prime Minister. However, in 2017 there were key elections in both France and Germany—the two countries that are at the core of the EU. In France, Marine Le Pen campaigned on France leaving the euro, and were she to score an upset victory, the euro would likely come under intense pressure. In Germany, Chancellor Angela Merkel's popularity had been hurt by concerns over immigration and terrorism, and there was a risk the EU could lose its most powerful leader. Accordingly, there was a risk the EU could face its toughest challenge yet.

As noted in Chap. 9, political risks in Europe subsequently dissipated, as Emanuel Macron, a centrist who is a strong supporter of the EU, won a decisive victory in France. Nonetheless, it is too early to tell whether the forces of populism and nationalism have been blunted. The reason: Many non-traditional parties have increased their representation in various parts of the EU. In Germany, for example, Angela Merkel won a fourth term as Chancellor, but the Christian Democrats and Social Democratic Party (SPD) both lost a large number of seats in parliament, and a far-right party won representation for the first time in the post-war era.

Are Expectations Too High?

Weighing these considerations, my assessment at the beginning of 2017 was there were valid reasons to believe the US economy would accelerate somewhat in the next couple of years as a result of favorable cyclical forces. Namely, the US economy began 2017 with improved momentum, confidence readings for US businesses and consumers were high and conditions abroad were improving.

However, the risk was that investor expectations for a pickup in the long-term trend growth rate were too high. The reason: Powerful secular forces stemming from low productivity growth and diminished labor force participation rates created significant headwinds. In my view, the best that could be hoped for was that tax and regulatory reform might boost trend growth by a quarter of one percentage point, but it was unrealistic to expect that the former trend rate of 3% would be restored. My assessment was in line with a survey of investor expectations by Cornerstone Research that was taken in June 2017.

While the Cornerstone survey suggests that investor expectations are reasonable, it should be noted that as of mid-2017, there was still an unusually large gap between so-called soft data that are based on expectations and "hard data" about the economy (Fig. 1.3). This suggested the stock market could be vulnerable to a pullback if economic growth did not accelerate in the next year or two.

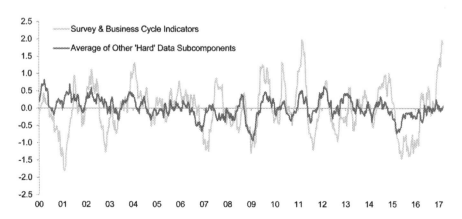

Fig. 1.3 "Hard" versus "soft" economic data: a large gap. (Source: Citigroup, Morgan Stanley Research)

How Will Markets Respond to Policy Changes?

Following the election there was a clear pattern to the way financial markets reacted initially—namely, US equities surged, Treasury bond yields spiked about 100 basis points and the dollar appreciated against a basket of currencies. These moves were all consistent with expectations of stronger economic growth, and they were dubbed "the Trump Trade."

Looking ahead, my assessment of how markets would ultimately play out depended on which set of economic policies prevailed. For this purpose I divided policies into three buckets: "Good policies" such as tax and regulatory reforms that equity investors would like, "Bad policies" that would result in outsized budget and trade deficits and which are likely to boost bond yields and "Ugly policies" such as protectionism that would undermine the global economy and investor confidence. These policies are covered in Chaps. 3, 4, 5, 6, 7, 8, and 9, which contain discussions of topics relating to the federal budget, healthcare reform, tax policy, regulatory policy, monetary policy, trade and exchange rate policy, and globalization and its impact on income distribution.

My conclusion was the best outcome for financial markets is one in which Congress passes corporate tax reform that will keep the budget and trade deficits within reasonable ranges. Investors will also favor efforts to lessen the regulatory burden businesses face, but as discussed in Chap. 6 it is inherently difficult to quantify the impact on the US economy. By contrast, the worst outcome would be an unnecessary trade war that threatened the global economy.

My assessment as Trump assumed office was the most likely outcome would fall somewhere in the middle—namely, Congress would enact tax cuts, but the tax base would not be broadened sufficiently to prevent the budget deficit from rising significantly in the next few years due to added financing burdens as baby boomers retire. Consequently, I expected financial market volatility to increase as investors altered their expectations about economic policies and the economy.

In a commentary for the first quarter of 2017, I summarized how our firm, Fort Washington Investment Advisors, viewed economic and financial conditions as follows[6]:

> the weight of evidence suggests the US economy and those abroad are experiencing the first synchronized expansion since the start of this decade. Financial conditions also remain favorable for growth and risk assets, even with the Federal Reserve raising interest rates.

Our investment strategy then was to maintain an overweight position in investment-grade and high-yield corporate bonds relative to treasuries. We also maintained our equity allocations, but we were steadily upgrading the overall

---

[6] Nicholas Sargen, Fort Washington Investment Advisors, Inc., First Quarter Commentary, "The Trump Rally at an Inflection Point," April, 2017.

quality of our portfolios in anticipation that market volatility would likely increase at some point.

The biggest surprise throughout 2017 was how well the stock market (and other risk assets) performed and how low market volatility remained, even though no major legislation was passed until late December. For some observers, this represents clear evidence that Trump's election was a game-changer for the stock market, although the verdict is out for the long-term performance of the economy. My own take is that the election was certainly a catalyst for the stock market; however, the rally was a worldwide phenomenon. This suggests other forces were at play—notably the impact of a synchronized expansion that boosted profits globally. Therefore, a lot is riding on how the rest of world fares, as it will impact US performance.

As 2018 began, one of the key issues for investors was whether the Trump administration and GOP could gain traction on the legislative front following passage of the tax bill. My own view was the Republicans would face formidable headwinds ahead of the 2018 mid-term elections, because of the political rancor that had been created and indications that they would have difficulty maintaining control of both houses of Congress. While there was talk in Republican circles of moving on to infrastructure spending and entitlement reform, the prospects for passing major legislation appeared low. Chapter 10 examines how long the rally in risk assets is likely to continue in these circumstances, as well as what investors need to consider in formulating their investment strategies for the remainder of the Trump era and beyond.

CHAPTER 2

Challenges to Restoring Long-Term Economic Growth

One of the most important issues in the 2016 elections related to the slowdown in US economic growth following the 2008 Global Financial Crisis (GFC) and what, if anything, can be done about it. The experience over the past decade was the worst in many peoples' lifetimes, and it contributed to anger and resentment that gave rise to populist movements around the world. The tendency for many is to point fingers at politicians, Wall Street, policymakers and the media for causing the problem or exacerbating it, rather than to look dispassionately about what happened.

Among economists there has been soul-searching about what went wrong, why they did not foresee the crisis and what needs to be done to rectify the situation. However, unlike the Great Depression, when John Maynard Keynes altered thinking away from classical economics toward greater government involvement, no new paradigm has emerged. This chapter, therefore, presents several competing views by prominent economists about the sources of slower growth and policies that have been proposed to rectify the situation:

- The first view asserts the growth slowdown is a hangover from excessive debt creation that led to the GFC. Research by Carmen Reinhart and Vincent Reinhart shows how the fallout fits the profile of many other financial crises, in which economic growth on average is a full percentage point below its prior trend.[1]
- The second view contends the United States and other economies are experiencing "secular stagnation." This thesis, as articulated by Larry Summers, explains why advanced economies have failed to respond to record low interest rates, and it contends real (inflation adjusted) interest rates may have to be negative to encourage capital formation.

---

[1] See Carmen Reinhart and Vincent Reinhart, "After the Fall," NBER Working Paper no. 16334, September 2010.

© The Author(s) 2018
N. P. Sargen, *Investing in the Trump Era*,
https://doi.org/10.1007/978-3-319-76045-2_2

- The third view is the economy's potential growth rate has slowed as a result of aging demographics and lower productivity growth. It is identified with Robert Gordon, an acknowledged expert on productivity, who cites headwinds that are likely to keep economic growth well below its former trend rate.[2]
- The fourth and final view maintains the root of the problem is excessive government intervention in the economy, rather than market failure. This view is popular among market-oriented economists, and a leading proponent is John Taylor.

This chapter synthesizes the above findings and offers my perspective about why US businesses may not respond as expected to prospective policy changes of the Trump administration. At the same time, I acknowledge it is too early to form definitive conclusions, and I cite several encouraging developments. My advice, therefore, is for people to be open minded on the issue.

Excessive Debt Creation as the Primary Cause

Throughout the post-war era until the start of the new millennium, the US economy sustained an average compound growth rate of more than 3% per annum. Whenever the economy would slip into recession, it would generally experience a "V-shaped" recovery, and steep declines were followed by sharp rebounds.

This pattern, however, did not unfold following the 2008 crisis: The US economy suffered its worst decline since the Great Depression, yet it experienced only a gradual recovery. Within the financial arena, Bill Gross and Mohammed El Arian of Pacific Investment Management Company (PIMCO) put forth the idea of the "New Normal."[3] Their contention was that the growth of the US economy in the post-war era was tied to excessive debt creation, and they argued that going forward US households and businesses would have to reduce their debt dependency (see Fig. 2.1). Their conclusion was that trend economic growth would be lower, most likely in the vicinity of 1.5% per annum.

A similar argument was put forth by Richard Koo of Nomura based on Japan's experience following the bursting of the real estate and stock market bubbles in the early 1990s.[4] Koo argued that Japan experienced a "balance sheet" recession, in which the top priority of companies was to reduce excessive levels of debt, which inhibited economic recovery. He also contended the

---

[2] See Robert Gordon, "The Turtle's Progress: Secular Stagnation Meets the Headwinds," *Secular Stagnation: Facts, Causes and Cures*, edited by Coen Teulings and Richard Baldwin, CEPR Press, Nov. 2014.

[3] Bill Gross, "On the Course to a New Normal," PIMCO Investment Outlook, September 2009.

[4] Richard Koo, *The Holy Grail of Macroeconomics: Lessons from Japan's Great Recession*, John Wiley, revised edition, August 2009.

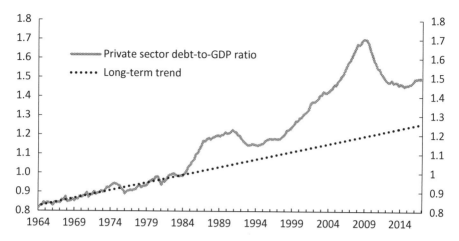

Fig. 2.1 US private sector debt buildup. (Source: Bank for International Settlements and US Bureau of Economic Analysis)
Trend based on average ratio for 1964–1984

United States is experiencing a similar phenomenon after the bursting of the housing bubble-spawned instability in the financial system.

Support for these views was provided by Carmen Reinhart and Vincent Reinhart in their study, "After the Fall."[5] They examined the 1929 stock market crash, the 1973 oil shock and the 2007 subprime collapse, as well as 15 other countries that experienced severe financial crises in the post-World War II era. Their principal finding is that real per capita GDP growth rates were significantly lower—on the order of a full percentage point per annum—during the decade following severe financial crises. At the same time, unemployment rates in the developed economies studied rose on average by five percentage points.

Viewed from these perspectives, the slowdown in economic growth following the 2008 financial crisis can be interpreted as a typical response to the bursting of a financial bubble. The remedy for avoiding a repeat is that policymakers need to be attuned to situations in which there is excessive buildup of debt. Unfortunately, this is easier said than done: There have been an increasing number of financial crises in the past four decades; yet policymakers typically are slow to act until after a bubble has burst and the financial system is threatened.[6]

Regarding policy prescriptions to counter post-crisis weakness, Keynesian-oriented economists have argued for increased government spending on a permanent, rather than temporary, basis. In his analysis of Japan's experience, for example, Richard Koo contended increased government spending was critical

---

[5] Reinhart and Reinhart, op. cit.
[6] See Sargen, op. cit., for a discussion of post-war asset bubbles and financial crises.

to offset weak spending by households and businesses. One critique of this argument, however, is that Japan undertook massive fiscal stimulus that boosted the ratio of public debt to GDP from 50% in 1980 to 250% recently, yet Japan's economy has not returned to its former growth trend.

In the United States, a public spending bill of close to $800 billion was enacted by the Obama administration in 2009, and some prominent economists including Paul Krugman contended much more needed to be done. However, there was a voter backlash during the 2010 mid-term elections, in which Republicans gained control of the House of Representatives and the Tea Party became a political force to block government spending. At the same time, many European countries with high levels of indebtedness were forced to embark on austerity programs, where the goal was to reduce debt ratios over time.

One of the conclusions of a study by Reinhart, Reinhart and Rogoff titled "Debt Overhangs: Past and Present" is that debt overhangs following financial crises can last a long time: Among the 26 episodes examined, 20 lasted more than a decade, and across all the cases, the average duration is about 23 years.[7] Moreover, the cumulative shortfall in output from debt overhang is potentially massive: "We find that growth effects are significant even in the many episodes where debtor countries were able to secure continued access to capital markets at relatively low real interest rates." The bottom line is that Keynesian pump priming may be feasible when public debt is relatively low, as it was during the Great Depression, but this is no longer the case today in most countries.

WEAK BUSINESS INVESTMENT AND THE "SECULAR STAGNATION" THESIS

Another perspective on the growth slowdown is that the United States and other developed economies are suffering from "secular stagnation." A leading proponent is Larry Summers, who in late 2013 resurrected the term that Alvin Hansen of Harvard used in the late 1930s to characterize economic conditions in which businesses were reluctant to invest even when interest rates were at record low levels.[8] The context for Summers' analysis was the Federal Reserve, Bank of Japan (BOJ) and European Central Bank (ECB) had reduced interest rates to zero while injecting massive amounts of reserves into the respective banking systems, and the BOJ and ECB were contemplating implementing negative interest rates. Despite this, the US economic expansion was unusually slow, and Japan and several countries in Europe experienced "double-dip" recessions.

---

[7] Carmen M. Reinhart, Vincent R. Reinhart, Kenneth S. Rogoff, "Debt Overhangs: Past and Present," NBER Working Paper 18105, April 2012.

[8] See Lawrence Summers, "U.S. Economic Prospects: Secular Stagnation, Hysteresis, and the Zero Lower Bound," *Business Economics* 49(2), 2014.

These circumstances caused Summers and other prominent economists to ask why aggressive monetary policies had failed to narrow the perceived wide gap between actual output and potential output. The main insight is that low real interest rates normally would be expected to boost investment demand relative to savings; however, this was not the case during the Great Depression or following the 2008 crisis. Summers stated it as follows:

> Hence the possibility exists that no attainable interest rate will permit the balancing of saving and investment at full employment. This is the secular stagnation hypothesis first put forward by Alvin Hansen in the 1930s. Notice that as Keynes, Tobin, and subsequently Brad Delong and I have emphasized, wage and price flexibility may well exacerbate the problem. The more flexible wages and prices are, the more they will be expected to fall during an output slowdown, leading to an increase in real interest rates. Indeed, there is the possibility of destabilizing deflation, with falling prices leading to higher real interest rates leading to greater output shortfalls leading to more rapidly falling prices and onwards in a vicious cycle.[9]

Summers goes on to present reasons that the full-employment real interest rate level has declined substantially. They include the following: (i) Slower population and possibly technological growth mean a reduction in the demand for new capital goods to equip new or more productive workers; (ii) lower-priced capital goods mean a given level of saving can purchase much more capital than was previously the case; (iii) rising income inequality raises the share of income going to people with a lower propensity to spend; (iv) greater risk aversion following the financial crisis and increased regulatory burdens drive a wedge between safe liquid assets and rates charged to borrowers; (v) a desire to accumulate reserves by central banks and sovereigns increases demand for safe assets, driving down their rates; and (vi) ongoing disinflation means that for any given real interest rate, real after-tax rates are higher.

Summers concludes by considering two possible strategies for addressing the problem of secular stagnation. One is for central banks to reduce real interest rates by raising their inflation targets from the customary 2% rate or by deploying quantitative easing that will reduce credit or term premiums. Another is to increase investment demand of the public sector: Summers, for example, has been an advocate for increased spending on public infrastructure.

Has US Potential Growth Slowed?

An alternative explanation for the growth slowdown is that it mainly stems from supply-side rather than demand-side considerations. A leading proponent is Robert Gordon, an acknowledged expert on US productivity, who contends the growth slowdown became apparent around the turn of the new

[9] See Lawrence Summers, "Reflections on the 'New Secular Stagnation Hypothesis,'" edited by Teulings and Baldwin, op. cit, p. 32.

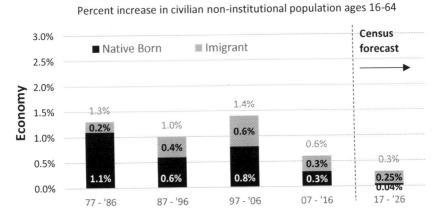

Percent increase in civilian non-institutional population ages 16-64

Fig. 2.2   Growth in the working-age populace (ages 16–64). (Source: Census Bureau, JPMorgan)

millennium.[10] Using 2007 as a starting point, he forecasts US economic growth will be well below its former trend rate and most likely between 1.4% and 1.6% per annum in the next decade.

One reason that is widely acknowledged is the significant slowing in the working-age population (16–64 years) to 0.6% per annum in the past decade from a trend rate of 1.2% previously (Fig. 2.2). This development is primarily the result of the aging of the US populace, as well as due to a slowing in the rate of immigration in the past decade. According to the Census Bureau, moreover, growth of the working-age populace is likely to decelerate further in the coming decade.

The more controversial issue is that some economists have contended Gordon's assessment is unduly pessimistic about the rate of technological change remaining close to 1% per annum. However, in a recent article Gordon counters that he assumes the pace of technological change will continue at a rate similar to that of the past four decades. In his view, the United States enjoyed a "productivity miracle" from the 1920s into the early 1970s, when growth in total factor productivity surged, but it has since fallen back to a more normal pace (See Fig. 2.3).

Instead, Gordon identifies four headwinds that are the sources of the growth slowdown—namely, demographics, education, income inequality and government debt. With respect to demographics, he notes that the slowdown in productivity growth that began in the 1970s was partly offset by rising labor force participation by females and baby-boomer teenagers who entered the labor force. Since 2007, however, labor force participation has fallen considerably due to the aging of the population as baby boomers retire and due to weak

---

[10] See Robert Gordon, "The Turtle's Progress: Secular Stagnation Meets the Headwinds," in Teulings and Baldwin, op. cit.

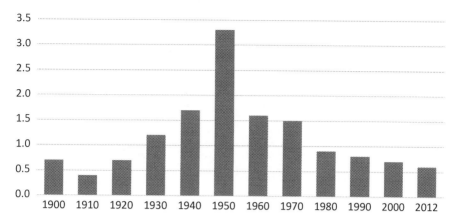

Fig. 2.3 Annual growth rates of total factor productivity (10 years preceding) in %. (Source: Robert J. Gordon Estimates)

economic conditions that discouraged people from staying in the work force. While some people may reenter the labor force if economic conditions continue to improve, the economy still faces the headwind of an aging population.

The second headwind is education. Gordon observes that rising high-school completion rates improved the productive potential of US workers throughout most of the twentieth century, but this transition was largely complete by 1970. The third headwind is rising income inequality. Gordon contends it is difficult to detect any growth in disposable (after tax) incomes for all but the super wealthy. (This issue is addressed in Chap. 9). In this regard, Gordon's assessment is similar to that of Summers.

The fourth headwind is the steady upward creep in the ratio of federal government debt to GDP. Gordon believes the official Congressional Budget Office (CBO) projections understate the gravity of the budgetary problem confronting the United States, because in his view the estimates of potential growth that are incorporated (1.8% per annum) are too high. (Note: This issue is discussed in greater depth in Chap. 3).

Gordon concludes his analysis by considering what, if anything, can be done to restore long-term growth. His message is there are no quick or easy fixes[11]:

> The Economist of 19 July 2014 got it right. America is riding on a slow-moving turtle. There is little politicians can do about it....
> The headwinds that are slowing the pace of the US's future economic growth have been decades in the making, entrenched in many aspects of our society. The reduction of inequality and the eradication of roadblocks in our educational system defy the cure-all of any legislation signed at the stroke of a pen. Innovation, even at the pace of 1972-2014, cannot overcome the ongoing momentum of the headwinds.

[11] Ibid, pp. 57–58.

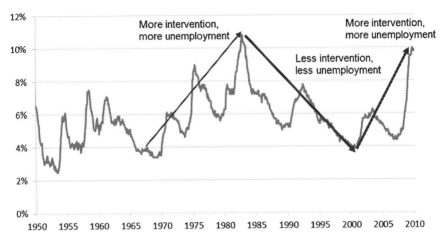

Fig. 2.4 Timelines of interventionism and unemployment. (Source: John Taylor)

INTERVENTIONIST GOVERNMENT POLICIES AS THE PROBLEM

By and large, economists who have a market-oriented bent reject the preceding hypotheses about what has gone wrong. Instead, they point the finger at government policies that have interfered with the market mechanism and which have increased uncertainty for households and businesses. A leading proponent of this camp is John Taylor, who articulated his assessment in his book *First Principles: Five Keys to Restoring America's Prosperity.*[12]

Taylor begins his book by rejecting the idea that the 2008 financial crisis and ensuing Great Recession were the result of market failure, as liberal economists assert. He writes[13]:

> Some people say that the financial crisis and the deep recession were caused by inherent failures of the market system, or at least too much reliance on that system. But the facts and timing readily available in the historical record show that certain government actions and interventions that preceded the crisis are much more the probable cause.

Taylor illustrates this point by showing a chart of the US unemployment rate from 1950 through the early part of this decade (see Fig. 2.4) Overlaying it are arrows that depict whether government intervention is rising, as in the period from the late 1960s to 1980 and the period from 2000 to 2010, as well as an arrow that points to less intervention during the era of Presidents Reagan, Bush and Clinton.

[12] John B. Taylor, *First Principles: Five Keys to Restoring America's Prosperity*, W.W. Norton & Company, 2013.
[13] Ibid, p. 16

Among the policies he cites that contributed to the 2008 financial crisis and subsequent growth slowdown are actions of the Federal Reserve that were highly unstable and unpredictable[14]:

> My own research showed that the low interest rates set by the Fed in 2003-2005 accelerated the housing-price boom, and thus led to the large housing bust. It also led to risk-taking as investors and financial institutions searched for higher yields.

In Taylor's opinion, a more rules-based federal funds rate would have prevented much of the housing boom and bust. (Note: This is an issue that is discussed in greater detail in Chap. 7).

With respect to fiscal policies, Taylor contends that tax rebates and onetime payments to households in 2001 and 2008 favored by Keynesian economists did little to jump-start the economy. He is a proponent of tax reform that simplifies the tax code and which includes measures to broaden the tax base in order to lessen the risk that the federal deficit will balloon. (Note: This issue is discussed in greater detail in Chap. 5). Instead, he sees many of the fiscal packages that have been implemented in the past two decades as having increased the national debt, which increases uncertainty about how it will be paid off.

IMPLICATIONS FOR FUTURE GROWTH

The respective hypotheses have varying implications for future economic growth. The central message of the Reinhart and Reinhart analysis is that financial crises are preceded by rapid debt accumulation in the private sector, and it generally takes a lengthy period to work the debt overhang down to manageable levels. The primary determinant of how long it takes to recover from a financial crisis is the speed of response to it.

The good news in the case of the United States is that businesses adjusted very rapidly to the crisis, by shedding labor and paring back capital spending. While these forces contributed to a severe recession, they also enabled profit growth to be restored within a matter of several years. As a result, companies and financial institutions were able to bolster their balance sheets fairly quickly. The same has been true of US households, who pared down debt service relative to income by boosting their saving rates and in some instances by receiving debt relief on their mortgages, as well as refinancing at lower interest rates (see Fig. 2.5). Consequently, the US economy has experienced a steady, albeit gradual, expansion since mid-2009.

The adjustment process has been slower in Europe, which has lagged the US economy. More recently, the EU economies have experienced their best growth in years, and this has helped boost corporate profits and European equity markets. By comparison, China experienced a massive debt buildup fol-

---

[14] Ibid, p. 44.

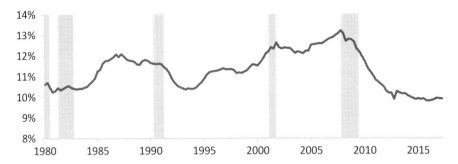

Fig. 2.5 US household debt service relative to disposable income. (Source: Board of Governors of the Federal Reserve System (US))

lowing the 2008 crisis, as the government sought to boost domestic demand to counter a slowing in export growth. While the Chinese economy continues to be the fastest growing in the world, economic growth nonetheless has fallen from double digits to 6% recently, and it is expected to slow further in coming years.

The main implication of the secular stagflation thesis is that real interest rates should be kept at low or even negative levels for years to come in order to revive business investment. One way to achieve this would be for central banks to raise their inflation targets to 3–4%. However, the Federal Reserve is not prepared to heed this advice, and it has begun the process of normalizing interest rates.

The most pessimistic view is that of Robert Gordon, as it implies a prolonged period of relatively low US economic growth. Also, Gordon does not offer any policy prescriptions that provide a quick improvement. His message is America needs to improve the quality of education for the masses, as well as the distribution of income, which will take years to yield results.

Finally, the most upbeat view is that of John Taylor, who believes subpar US expansion is mainly attributable to government intervention. He cites the policies of the Reagan administration as a road map of what should be done to reinvigorate the US economy.

THE TRUMP ADMINISTRATION AND CONGRESSIONAL REPUBLICAN AGENDA

One of my purposes in discussing these views is to illustrate there is no consensus among academic economists about what went wrong after the 2008 financial crisis and what needs to be done to rectify the situation.

To a large extent, the difference in views reflects whether the respective economists favor increased government involvement in the economy or less involvement. One of the critical issues on the policy front is whether the slowdown is perceived to be the result of diminished aggregate demand (such as the debt overhang or secular stagnation views), supply-side constraints related to aging demographics and diminished productivity growth, or government intervention that impedes the private sector. That said, there is general agreement that a fundamental growth slowdown occurred before and after the GFC, and policymakers face significant challenges trying to restore economic growth to the former trend rate.

The proposals being put forth by the Trump administration and Republican leadership in Congress fall squarely in the market-oriented camp. Government involvement in the economy during the Obama years is viewed as inhibiting market forces, and the policies the Trump administration and Republican leadership are proposing are intended to unleash the economy's productive potential by lowering corporate tax rates, allowing immediate deduction of capital outlays and lessening regulatory burdens of businesses.

While financial markets have greeted the proposals enthusiastically, most economists are cautious about their ability to boost economic growth significantly. According to a *Wall Street Journal* survey of 59 economists, forecasters on average think long-term GDP growth could rise to 2.3% per annum, a 0.3% increase from their 2.0% baseline, while unemployment would average 4.4% instead of 4.5%.[15] The bottom line is economic forecasters see a modest improvement in the coming decade, but considerably less than what the Trump administration is banking on.

Because changes in productivity trends are evident only after long periods of time, it is important for investors to have gauges to discern whether policies are moving the needle in the right direction. In this regard, surveys of consumer and business confidence clearly indicate optimism about the direction of policy changes being contemplated. From my perspective, the most important is the National Federation of Independent Business (NFIB) survey of small businesses, which is correlated with overall economic performance. It has shown a significant jump in confidence readings since the election (see Fig. 2.6). As NFIB Chief Economist Bill Dunkelberg observed[16]:

We've been doing this research for nearly half a century, longer than anyone else, and I've never seen anything like 2017…The 2016 election was like a dam breaking. Small business owners were waiting for better policies from Washington, suddenly they got them, and the engine of the economy roared back to life.

In the meantime I believe investors should focus on business investment as the critical gauge of whether the policies of the Trump administration and the Republican-controlled Congress are having their intended impact. The reason: Most economists consider sluggish business investment to be the main factor contributing to the subdued economic expansion. There is also general agreement that a revival of business investment is important to improving productivity growth.

[15] Wall Street Journal, May 12, 2007, p. 2.
[16] NFIB Research Foundation, December 2017 Report: "Average Monthly Optimism Sets All-Time Record High in 2017."

Fig. 2.6 NFIB survey of small businesses optimism index. (Source: NFIB)

My own assessment on this matter differs from most observers who believe the reluctance of businesses to invest in plant and equipment reflects undue caution on their part. Rather, I contend that in the aftermath of the 2008 financial crisis, the overriding objective of US businesses was to restore profitability, which had plummeted by 50%. The US companies did so initially by shredding workers in droves and by halting capital spending plans. Over time, as the economy and financial system stabilized, they began to hire workers, which they viewed as a variable cost, while holding back on capital spending. Subsequently, their profit margins began to rise to record levels and their share prices surged along with it. In the process US businesses learned the recipe for how to make money in a subpar economic environment, and investors rewarded them for doing so. In this respect, the US experience is the diametric opposite of Japan's.

In this context, it is unclear whether US businesses will boost capital outlays in response to cuts in the corporate tax rate, accelerated depreciation allowances and lessened regulatory burdens. My take is they will be inclined to wait for wage pressures to build and profit margins to shrink before they are compelled to boost spending on plant and equipment. That said, there is no precedent to be confident about how businesses will respond. Therefore, people need to be open minded about the prospective outcome.

Conclusion: The Slowdown Is a Global Phenomenon

Finally, while the issue of sluggish economic growth was one of the focal points of the 2016 elections, it is important to recognize the United States is by no means alone. Indeed, virtually every advanced economy and most developing economies have experienced slowdowns in the aftermath of the GFC. In fact, when viewed from a global perspective, the US economy has outperformed the European economies and Japan considerably, and the restoration of US corporate profits is a key reason for the outperformance of the US stock market.

Nonetheless, the tendency for voters is to blame the party in power when economic conditions are not as strong as they once were.

The second observation is that most advanced economies are beginning to normalize a decade after the onset of the GFC. One reason why global equity markets were surprisingly robust in 2017 is the global economy experienced a synchronized expansion for the first time since 2010. This is discussed in Chap. 10.

Third, President Trump and the Republican leadership in Congress are pinning their hopes for reviving growth on tax reform and diminished government intervention in the economy. This is a sensible response and one of the reasons for investor optimism. Nonetheless, for reasons cited it remains to be seen whether such policies will be implemented and, if so, whether they will prove to be effective.

PART II

Fiscal and Regulatory Policies
to Promote Growth

CHAPTER 3

Assessing the US Fiscal Imbalance: Why It Matters

One issue that was not discussed in any depth during the 2016 election is the state of the federal government's finances, a subject that traditionally has been important for the Republican Party. To be sure, Republican candidates criticized the Obama administration for a massive buildup in federal debt from 2009 through 2016 (see Fig. 3.1). The response from Democrats was that it was a legacy from the 2008 crisis during the Bush administration, and Donald Trump's proposals for the budget would cause it to balloon considerably more. Beyond this give-and-take, the issue of the sustainability of federal finances was ignored, and there was no sense of urgency about the problem.

One reason may be "debt fatigue." When Republicans gained control of the House of Representatives in 2010, Tea Party members routinely blocked passage of federal budgets to control government spending. At one point, the government shut down temporarily, and a series of continuing resolutions had to be passed to keep it in business. Over time, as the electorate grew weary of political gridlock, the stage was set for Trump, an outspoken critic of Washington with no apparent political philosophy, to win the Republican nomination.

The backdrop for the election was also one in which government finances had improved, with the ratio of the federal deficit to GDP within a normal bound of 2–3% (see Fig. 3.2). Nonetheless, the landscape is about to worsen considerably beginning in the next few years. The reason: As the generation of baby boomers retires, increased burdens will be placed on entitlement programs such as Social Security, Medicare and Medicaid. Indeed, according to the CBO, the federal budget deficit is projected to climb to 5% of GDP over the coming decade. If this scenario were to unfold, it would imply the ratio of federal debt held by the public to GDP would approach the all-time high during World War II by the end of the next decade.

This chapter explores several issues relating to these matters. First, how did the budgetary situation become so tenuous? Second, how will policies of the Trump administration and Congressional Republicans alter the outlook? Third,

© The Author(s) 2018
N. P. Sargen, *Investing in the Trump Era*,
https://doi.org/10.1007/978-3-319-76045-2_3

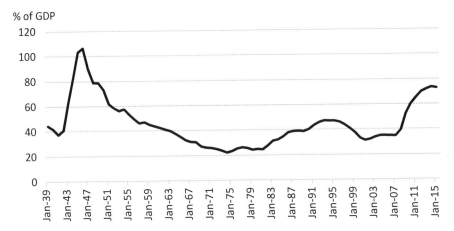

Fig. 3.1   Federal debt held by the public. (Source: U.S. Treasury)

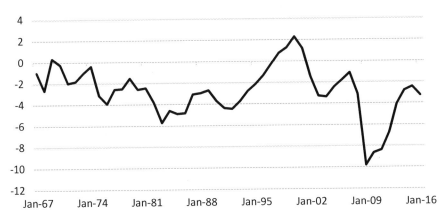

Fig. 3.2   Federal budget deficit as a percent of GDP. (Source: U.S. Treasury)

what risks are entailed for the economy and financial markets if the budgetary picture does not improve? Fourth, what policy options can be taken to lessen the risks?

The Evolution of America's Budgetary Problems

For the first 20 years or so following World War II, the United States was a beacon of fiscal rectitude. The economy grew at a 3½% annual rate, which boosted government revenues, and together with cutbacks in military spending after the war, the federal budget was close to being balanced much of the time. Consequently, the ratio of publicly held federal debt outstanding relative to GDP fell from a high of more than 100% of GDP during World War II to 30% in the mid-1960s.

The transition to chronic budget deficits began in the second half of the 1960s, when the Johnson administration implemented a strategy to fund both the Vietnam War and Great Society programs that entailed deficit financing. Economists at the time called the strategy "guns and butter." Thereafter, the budget imbalance rose to 4% of GDP by the early 1990s, after averaging about 2% of GDP over two-and-a-half decades. The main outlier occurred during the Reagan years, when the imbalance reached a peak of 5% of GDP in response to tax cuts and increased spending for both military and social programs.

During the Clinton years, the pattern reversed temporarily, as budget deficits declined steadily and by the latter part of the 1990s the United States ran budgetary surpluses. The goal of both President Clinton and Treasury Secretary Robert Rubin was to reduce high government bond yields through deficit-reduction measures, which proved successful. In addition, the budgetary situation benefitted from the boom in technology, which boosted labor productivity and US economic growth accelerated to 4%. These developments, in turn, helped to swell the government's coffers.

Indicative of the optimism at the time, Federal Reserve Chairman Alan Greenspan testified to Congress that the government would soon be able to shrink the size of its outstanding debt and that this could contribute to a shortage of government bonds for investors.[1] Greenspan's analysis factored in forecasts of both the CBO and the OMB, which assumed productivity growth in the next decade would average between 2¼% and 2½%, which was above the long-term trend but below the average of the previous five years:

> The most recent projections, granted their tentativeness, nonetheless make clear that the highly desirable goal of paying off the federal debt is in reach before the end of the decade.[2]

Greenspan went on to contemplate the possibility that, as federal debt outstanding was paid off, the government at some point would need to consider accumulating large quantities of private assets. He also endorsed the idea that future budget surpluses be lowered by tax reductions (which the Bush administration proposed at the time) rather than spending increases. He concluded his testimony by acknowledging the uncertainties in the economic and budget outlook, and ended with a cautionary note[3]:

> With today's euphoria surrounding the surpluses, it is not difficult to imagine the hard-earned fiscal restraint developing in recent years rapidly dissipating. We need to resist those policies that could readily resurrect the deficits of the past and the fiscal imbalances that followed in their wake.

---

[1] Testimony of Chairman Alan Greenspan, "Outlook for the federal budget and implications for fiscal policy," before the Senate Budget Committee, January 25, 2001.
[2] Ibid.
[3] Ibid.

Just two months later circumstances began to change dramatically. In the wake of the bursting of the technology bubble that began in March 2000, the economy began to soften, and it eventually slipped into mild recession around the time of 9/11. These developments together with tax cuts implemented under the Bush administration caused federal revenues to decline while government spending increased. As a result, the federal deficit shifted back into deficit, and optimism about budgetary surpluses was dealt a swift blow.

As noted previously, the most important factor that contributed to the ballooning of the budget deficit from 2008 onward was the GFC and Great Recession. The Bush administration responded by authorizing a $700 billion Troubled Asset Relief Program (TARP) that was eventually used to recapitalize large banks and other financial institutions. This was followed by a fiscal stimulus package of close to $800 billion under the Obama administration that was enacted to save jobs, create new jobs and provide relief to those who were severely affected. The 2009 budget culminated in a deficit of $1.4 trillion, or nearly 10% of GDP, as the economy experienced its worst recession in the post-war era.

A political backlash in 2010 resulted in the Republican Party winning control of the House of Representatives, which brought in candidates who identified with the Tea Party wing. Thereafter, they sought to rein in the growth of federal spending by blocking passage of federal budgets, and annual budget deficits relative to GDP fell fairly steadily.

Amid the budgetary fluctuations over the past 50 years, two distinct patterns stand out. First, tax revenues as a percent of GDP have been fairly steady at about 18–19%, with variations linked to recessions or expansions. Second, government expenditures have increased from about 20–22%. Moreover, they are projected to rise considerably in the coming decade.

The Rise of Mandated Government Programs

Looking ahead, structural forces are at work that will make further deficit reduction difficult, and which raise the specter of much larger ones. They relate to (i) the steady increase in mandated government programs since the late 1960s and (ii) the aging of the US population.

The steady expansion in the portion of outlays to fund mandated programs such as Social Security, Medicare, Medicaid and interest on the national debt is shown in Fig. 3.3. When Medicare and Medicaid were launched in the 1960s, the U.S. population was relatively young, and mandated programs accounted for roughly 30% of total expenditures, while spending on discretionary items such as defense, education, the environment and social programs accounted for 70% of the total. Today, the situation is the exact opposite, with discretionary spending accounting for 30% of the pie and mandated programs for 70%.

This differential, moreover, is expected to continue widening in the years ahead as baby boomers retire and the population ages (Fig. 3.4). Currently, the ratio of workers to retirees covered by social security is about 2.8 times, down from 42 times in 1945. By the second half of this century, the ratio is projected

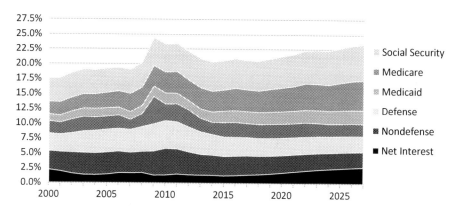

Fig. 3.3 Federal government spending and composition. (Note: Figures for 2017–2027 are forecasts. Source: Congressional Budget Office)

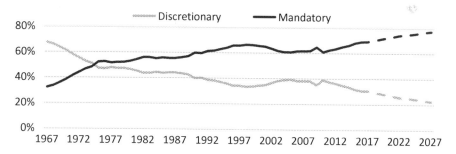

Fig. 3.4 Federal spending: mandated programs overtake discretionary spending. (Note: Figures for 2017–2027 are forecasts. Source: Congressional Budget Office)

to fall to about two times.[4] The aging of the population is a key reason the CBO is projecting a steady widening in the US budget imbalance beginning in the next few years. *If these projections come to fruition, mandated programs will account for all revenues of the federal government by the end of the next decade.* This means that outlays for discretionary programs will either have to be financed via increased taxes or through deficit financing.

The bottom line is the United States no longer has the luxury of time for a chronic fiscal imbalance to fix itself. Indeed, the day of fiscal reckoning may be approaching sooner than most people realize. As the CBO writes in *The Budget and Economic Outlook: 2017 to 2027*, the consequences of allowing the situation to unfold are likely to be felt in many ways:

> High and rising federal debt would reduce national saving and income in the long-term; increase the government's interest payments, thereby putting more pressure on the rest of the budget; limit lawmakers' ability to respond to unforeseen events; and increase the likelihood of a fiscal crisis.

[4] See Social Security Administration, Social Security Solvency, Annual Report.

Are CBO Projections Too Pessimistic?

Some commentators contend CBO budget deficit projections are too pessimistic, because they assume the recent growth trend of 1.9% will be maintained throughout the forecast period. By comparison, the latest budget projections by OMB are based on economic growth reverting to 3%, assuming the policies of the Trump administration are enacted successfully. As the discussion of the Clinton years suggests, this possibility cannot be ruled out. However, with labor force growth today considerably lower than in the 1990s, it would imply a significant improvement in labor productivity to achieve the growth target. Yet, as discussed in Chap. 2, there are considerable headwinds to achieve a revival in productivity.

Another consideration is how economic policies in the coming decade will alter the budgetary outlook. One of the biggest challenges investors face in this regard is the budgetary policies advocated by President Trump differ considerably from those of House Speaker Ryan and other Republican leaders in Congress. The key differences relate to entitlement programs and tax policy.

During the 2016 campaign Trump made a conscious decision not to challenge Hillary Clinton and the Democrats on the issue of entitlement programs. In contrast to House Speaker Paul Ryan and other Republican leaders in Congress, he vowed not to touch entitlement programs, while at the same time advocating increased government spending for defense and infrastructure. One modification Trump has made since becoming President is that he now favors a pullback of Medicaid expansion that was part of Obamacare.

If entitlement programs are not scaled back, an implication is that other areas of discretionary spending will have to be cut significantly to prevent a blowout of the budget. The extent was revealed in 2018 budget proposal submitted by OMB in May 2017: It called for extensive cutbacks in social programs such as Medicaid, food stamps, student loans, disability programs among others, as well as deep cuts in education and environmental programs.[5] Another possible victim is spending on infrastructure, which had been a priority of both Republicans and Democrats during the 2016 campaign, but which was barely mentioned following the outcome.[6] All told, the proposal calls for nondefense spending to fall to a historic low of 1.4% of GDP in 2026 from 3.5% in 2016.

The prospects for such sweeping changes being enacted by Congress were deemed to be low, however, as moderate Republicans viewed them as too extreme. One critique of the Trump administration's proposal was it did not specify how the cuts will be made. Instead, it set a "Two Penny" plan, which decreed that nondefense discretionary spending would fall by 2% per annum

---

[5] OMB, Budget of the US Government, "A New Foundation for American Greatness," FY 2018.

[6] Early on, there had been talk of funding increased infrastructure spending via public–private partnerships, but this was all but forgotten amid the turmoil over replacing Obamacare.

throughout the next decade. Most budget experts considered this to be a fantasy wish, and even moderate Republicans were quick to declare the proposal "dead on arrival."

A second key difference is the President is in favor of tax cuts, corporate and personal, that will boost the economy, whereas Speaker Ryan and the House leadership have advocated tax reform that broadens the tax base, so it is deficit neutral. (The distinction between tax cuts and tax reform is discussed in greater detail in Chap. 5.) The question then becomes: How will the tax cuts be paid?

The answer from President Trump and his economic advisers is that tax cuts will spur economic growth, which, in turn, will boost revenues. In short, they believe tax cuts will be self-financing. Yet they do not specify where the revenues will come. The same argument was made during the Reagan era, when tax cuts were lowered substantially during the first term, but then had to be partially unwound as the budget deficit ballooned. During the second term, tax reform legislation was enacted that enabled the economy to grow without ballooning the budget deficit further.

The bottom line is that President Trump's proposals to leave entitlements untouched (with a possible exception for Medicaid), boost spending on the military and infrastructure and cut tax rates significantly risked a much faster expansion of the budget deficit than is built into CBO projections. By comparison, the proposal contained in the House Republican bill drafted in the summer of 2016 would have less of a budgetary impact. However, as is discussed in Chap. 5, it contains provisions that are controversial and which are unlikely to be enacted. Therefore, a lot was riding on the specific provisions that are enacted into legislation.

ASSESSING BUDGETARY RISKS

Considering how long the US budget has been imbalanced and the massive buildup in federal debt over the past four decades, one may ask why we should be concerned now, especially when the deficit appears under control. Indeed, some observers have questioned whether deficits really matter.

The debate over the budget deficit and the role foreign institutions played in financing it was front and center in the middle of the past decade, when the budget deficit climbed to 4% of GDP, while the current account deficit surged to 6% of GDP. The United States had become a net debtor internationally, and the imbalances were mainly financed by purchases of US debt from China and other emerging Asian economies. By the mid-2000s, foreign institutions held close to 40% of outstanding Treasury debt, and several prominent luminaries including Paul Volcker, Robert Rubin, George Soros and Warren Buffett contended the imbalances were unsustainable and fraught with risks.

One of the ironies of the GFC is that the United States seemingly should have been vulnerable to capital flight considering that the crisis began with the problem in US housing and subprime loans. As the crisis unfolded, however, it became apparent how exposed many foreign institutions were to mortgage-backed securities and other structured products. As they sold off, overseas economies were impacted along with the United States. In the flight to quality that ensued, America was perceived to be a safe haven for investors, and a crisis in confidence was averted. This example illustrates the difficulty of trying to time when financial crises will occur, and then anticipating how they will play out.

The more likely outcome, in my view, is that outsized budget deficits and continued rapid accumulation of federal debt at some point will cause bond-holders to reassess risks. If so, it could result in higher bond yields than investors currently envision, which in turn could crowd out private investment.

Lawrence Goodman, president of the Center for Financial Stability who previously served at the US Treasury, contends the US debt situation is worse than most people realize.[7] In his view, the buildup in federal debt over the past decade is an accident waiting to happen. One reason: The Federal Reserve is poised to begin reducing the size of its $4.5 trillion balance sheet, which includes $2.5 trillion in US Treasury holdings. (Note: prior to the financial crisis the Fed's assets totaled less than $1 trillion.) To be sure, the Fed has gone out of its way to assure investors it will proceed gradually, so as not to disrupt markets. However, the reality is that no central bank has ever faced this situation before, so one cannot be sure how it will evolve.

Second, Goodman points out that Treasury debt is abnormally skewed to short-term maturities. This presents a problem, as the Treasury must be able to roll them over, when budget deficits are set to rise considerably. Goodman points out that in 2017 the Treasury had to roll over or refinance debt equivalent to 18% of GDP, compared with an average of 10% per year from 1973 to 2008. On top of this, it had to finance additional debt equivalent to 3% of GDP, which makes its total reliance on capital market financing equivalent to 21% of GDP. Over the period from 2017 to 2021, 70% of Treasury debt will have to be refunded from domestic and foreign borrowers.

The third type of risk arises because liquidity in the US bond market has declined considerably since the financial crisis. This means that investors who try to sell their holdings face much higher transactions costs than in the past. In the event of a general rise in interest rates, market illiquidity could add to problems.

POLICY OPTIONS

Weighing these considerations, there are several options for policymakers to consider to prevent a blowout of the federal deficit. One is to leave current policies in place and hope the problem will take care of itself. This, in effect, is

[7] Lawrence Goodman, "The National Debt Is a Bigger Problem than You Think," *The Fiscal Times*, June 6, 2017.

what has been happening for several decades without the United States suffering any major consequences. The problem, however, is the implied debt
buildup in the CBO projections indicate the situation is unsustainable and
fraught with risks.

A second option is to slow the growth of entitlement programs. While this
may be a sensible strategy, it is also risky for politicians, as elderly voters would
punish anyone who tampers with Social Security or Medicare. The route that
Congressional Republicans has pursued is to leave those two programs in place,
but to roll back the expansion of Medicaid that is a central part of Obamacare.

A third option is shrink the size of nondefense discretionary spending via
draconian cuts in various social programs. This is the strategy the Trump
administration pursued in its 2018 budget, but which was ultimately rejected
by Congress.

A fourth option is to leave entitlement and social programs in place, and to
pay for them with increased taxes on the wealthy. This was the strategy both
Hillary Clinton and Bernie Sanders campaigned on in the 2016 elections.
While it is unacceptable to Republicans, it could occur if the Democrats were
to win the Presidency and Congressional control in 2020.

Of these options, only one is a viable strategy over the long run. Namely,
reform of entitlement programs is necessary, as they ultimately are what makes
the budgetary situation unsustainable. Put simply, over the past five decades
the federal government has made commitments to the public that it can no
longer afford to keep. The reason: People are living longer today than was
assumed at the time the commitments were made, and program costs have
increased much faster than were anticipated.

That said, it is easier to reform the social security system than the healthcare
system. The main source of strain on the social security system, for example, is
longevity risk: That is, people today are living much longer (77 years for males
and nearly 82 years for females) than in 1940 (61 and 66 years, respectively)
when the system was just beginning (see Table 3.1). Also, assuming people
retire at 65, there is a much larger percentage that draw claims on the system
today. The average life expectancy for those who make it to 65 is another
18.4 years for males and 20.8 years for females today versus 11.9 years and
13.4 years in 1940.

Recognizing this, the most sensible way to put the system on firm actuarial
footings is to delay the date at which people are eligible to begin receiving full
benefits. In 1983, amendments to the Social Security Act were enacted that
phased in a gradual increase in the age for collecting full social security benefits
from 65 to 67 over a 22-year period. Alan Greenspan, who chaired the Social
Security Commission deliberations of 1983, gave the following testimony to
Congress in 1997, when he served as Chairman of the Federal Reserve:

As I argued at length during the Social Security Commission deliberations of
1983, with only modest effect, some delaying of the eligibility for retirement
benefits is becoming increasingly pressing. For example, adjusting the full-benefits

Table 3.1 Changing life expectancies

Changing life expectancies	Birth	Age 65
Male 1940	61.4	11.9
Male 2015	77.1	18.4
Male 2062	82.1	21.4
Female 1940	65.7	13.4
Female 2015	81.7	20.8
Female 2062	85.7	23.3

Source: Social Security Administrative Practice

retirement age further to keep pace with increases in life expectancy in a way that would keep the ratio of retirement years to expected life span approximately constant would significantly narrow the funding gap. Such an initiative would become easier to implement as fewer and fewer of our older citizens retire from previously arduous work. Hopefully, other modifications to social security, such as improved cost-of-living, will be instituted.[8]

By comparison, the challenges the government confronts in reforming the healthcare system and the Medicare and Medicaid programs are considerably greater. The main reason is that the problem of funding healthcare and putting it on a sound actuarial basis is much more complex: While some of the problems of rising expenditures are associated with the aging of the US population, medical costs have far outstripped consumer price inflation for five decades, and attempts to rein them in have failed. Furthermore, embedded in Obamacare was an expansion of eligibility for Medicaid recipients that is projected to add an additional $1 trillion in costs over the next ten years. These issues are examined in greater detail in Chap. 4.

Need for a Longer-Term Perspective

One of the inherent challenges of democratic rule is that voters are fixated on current problems, and politicians are pressured to come up with quick fixes to them. Most have concluded it is a mistake to try to educate the electorate about issues, and they must acquiesce to the will of the populace.

The last time there was a comprehensive discussion of issues pertaining to budgetary outlook over the medium–longer term was in 2010. President Obama created a presidential commission called the National Commission on Fiscal Responsibility and Reform to identify "policies to improve the fiscal situation in the medium term and to achieve fiscal sustainability over the long term." It received bipartisan support and was chaired Alan Simpson and Erskine Bowles, and became known as the Simpson-Bowles Plan.

[8] Testimony of Chairman Alan Greenspan, Social Security, before the Task Force on Social Security, US Senate Budget Committee, November 20, 1997.

The final plan contained six major components of savings totaling nearly $4 trillion covering the period from 2012 to 2020 that reduced the federal debt that had been projected in the CBO baseline forecast considerably over time. It including the following items: (i) discretionary spending cuts of $1.66 trillion, (ii) $1 trillion in added revenue from tax reform, (iii) $340 billion in healthcare savings, (iv) $215 billion in savings by changing the measure of inflation used to index payments, (v) $238 billion in Social Security reform and (vi) additional savings of $673 billion on interest payments associated with lower debt financing.

The plan was ultimately scrapped, because it fell short of a supermajority of the committee needed to pass it, even though a majority—11 of 18 votes—were in favor. While the plan received bipartisan support, four Democrats and three Republicans (Paul Ryan, Jeb Hensarling and Dave Camp) voted against it. Unfortunately, the prospect of reviving such a proposal today would be considered Dead on Arrival (DOA), given the deep political divide between Republicans and Democrats. A vivid illustration of how difficult it is to reach agreement occurred in the spring of 2012, when a budget resolution based in part on the Simpson-Bowles plan was voted on in the House of Representatives and was voted down 382–38. As Maya MacGuineas of the Committee for a Responsible Federal Budget observes:[9]

> The Commission released not only a credible plan, but an excellent plan. Of course it is filled with things people don't like—that is the nature of deficit reduction. And yet the plan received bipartisan support from a majority of the Commission at a time where, up until now, financial leadership has been in short supply.[10]

Policy Implications: Near Term and Longer Term

Americans face a choice in the years ahead about setting priorities for government spending and how to pay for government programs, whether out of taxes or via debt financing. Thus far, the implicit choices they have made are to increase the social safety net contained in entitlement programs but to delay paying for them by funding them via deficit finance. Thus far, it is hard to see any immediate repercussions of pursuing such a course, as America has been able to attract financing from abroad on very favorable terms.

Going forward, however, the key issue is whether this approach is sustainable as the number of retirees grows and the population ages and as federal debt outstanding reaches levels that may be unsustainable. If nothing is done to make entitlement programs actuarially sound, the risk is that investors will reassess the US budgetary situation at some point and financing costs will rise significantly. While no one can predict when this day will come, it is better to take action to lessen the risk of a loss of investor confidence than to allow the problem to fester indefinitely.

---

[9] Ezra Klein, "Wonkbook: House reaches bipartisan deal to reject Simpson-Bowles," The Washington Post, December 1, 2012.

[10] Committee for a Responsible Budget, "CFRB Commends the Excellent Work of the Fiscal Commission," December 1, 2012.

CHAPTER 4

What Makes Healthcare Reform So Complex: A Primer

Of all the issues in the 2016 election, the most contentious is related to healthcare insurance. Since the ACA was enacted without a single Republican vote in 2010, the Republican Party made it a priority to repeal Obamacare. Throughout the 2016 campaign Republican candidates stood united on this issue contending the ACA was failing, and upon assuming office, President Trump urged Congressional Republicans to enact legislation to repeal and replace it. Yet, to the amazement of many, Senate Republicans were unable to reach agreement, and the ACA remained the law of the land. Amid all this, President Trump famously declared, "Nobody knew healthcare could be so complicated."[1]

My goal in this chapter is to help people understand what makes healthcare so complex and contentious. To do so, one first needs to have a basic understanding of how the US system compares with those of other countries, and how it has evolved from a "fee for service" model of compensation to a system of managed care, in which people pay for bundled services. It is also important to grasp the reasons many doctors and patients are critical of managed care, especially health maintenance organizations (HMOs), while many healthcare analysts contend the system saves money and does not compromise health. The chapter also reviews the attempt to implement universal coverage during the Clinton administration and then takes up the controversy surrounding Obamacare and Republican opposition to it.

Following this review, we consider the primary goals of healthcare reform. Simply put, the challenge for policymakers is to find a solution that will balance each of three competing goals: (i) Assure increased access to health insurance, (ii) contain ratcheting medical costs and (iii) maintain the quality of healthcare. For much of the post-war era, the Democratic Party has sought to achieve affordable healthcare for all Americans, while the Republican Party has primarily been concerned with controlling skyrocketing healthcare costs. Along the way,

[1] CNNPolitics.com, February 28, 2017.

© The Author(s) 2018
N. P. Sargen, *Investing in the Trump Era*,
https://doi.org/10.1007/978-3-319-76045-2_4

however, quality of care became a third consideration in the wake of criticisms by doctors and patients over managed care. We conclude that the problem of finding an acceptable solution transcends political differences: It also reflects differences between various power centers including physicians, hospitals, insurers, pharmaceutical companies and employers. Even more basic is the issue of who will pay for the costs associated with expanded coverage.

Finally, amid the political drama over the repeal of Obamacare, we find there is little impact on the relative performance of healthcare stocks. This may be surprising considering the controversies during the Clinton and Obama administrations resulted in the healthcare sector materially underperforming the broad market. One explanation is the current debate is viewed by investors as mainly impacting insurance companies that provide coverage to a limited segment of the market, rather than affecting the broader healthcare sector.

US Healthcare: A Mixed System

One of the first things that is apparent about the US healthcare system is how different it is from most other advanced countries that have a universal system in which the government provides medical and hospital insurance coverage for all citizens. By comparison, the United States has a mixed system: The private sector provides close to two-thirds of total coverage—54% via employer plans and another 11% through individual participants, while the remainder is provided by the government through Medicare (16%), Medicaid (17%) and military-related programs (5%).[2]

A second distinguishing feature of the US healthcare system is how expensive it is in relation to other countries (see Table 4.1). Based on survey data compiled in 2013, spending on US healthcare relative to GDP was about 17% compared with a median of 10% for 16 other mostly advanced countries.[3] The survey also found the United States had the highest healthcare spend rate per capita ($9086 in 2013 and more than $10,000 in 2015), roughly twice the median amount for other advanced economies.

Despite this, various metrics such as life expectancy and quality of care do not show the US system has delivered superior outcomes. One area in which the US system scores well is in being the most innovative in terms of medical techniques and sophistication, which is why wealthy people from around the world come to the United States for medical treatment.

The survey, nonetheless, revealed considerable dissatisfaction with participants as a whole (see Table 4.2). Only one-quarter of respondents indicated the system worked well, while the remaining three-quarters reported it either

[2] See The Commonwealth Fund, The US Heath Care System, 2014.
[3] See 2015 *International Profile of Health Care Systems*, edited by Elias Mossialos and Marton Wenzel of the London School of Economics and Robin Osborn and Dana Sarnak of The Commonwealth Fund, January 2016.

Table 4.1   Healthcare system cost indicators (2013)

	16 countries		
	US	Median	Range
Healthcare spend			
Percentage of GDP	17.1%	10%	5.4% – 11.7%
Per capita ($)[a]	9086	4500	636 – 6,325
Out-of-pocket[a] per capita	1074	625	216 – 1,360
Hospital spend			
Per discharge ($)	20,991	–	2,033 – 14,408
Medical technology			
MRI exams (per 1k pop.)	106.9	–	27.6 – 90.9

Source: 2015 International Profiles of Healthcare System
[a]Adjusted for differences in cost of living

Table 4.2   Healthcare system quality indicators (2013)

	10 countries		
	US	Median	Range
Access to care			
Barrier due to cost	37%	13%	4% – 22%
OECD quality indicators			
Breast cancer 5 year survival	88.9%	–	81.1% – 89.8%
Mortality per myocardial infarction per 100 admission	5.5	6.7	4.1 – 8.7
Public views of health system			
Works well	25%	46%	40% – 63%
Fundamental changes needed	48%	45%	33% – 50%
Need to be rebuilt	27%	8%	4% – 12%

Source: 2015 International Profiles of Healthcare System

required fundamental change or needed to be rebuilt.[4] Among the biggest criticisms of the system are (i) a large number of Americans do not have any medical coverage, (ii) prior to Obamacare those that had coverage via their jobs were at risk of losing it when they switched jobs, (iii) medical costs have been growing at a rate that far outstrips the overall rate inflation and (iv) managed care has sacrificed quality of healthcare for cost savings.

EVOLUTION OF US HEALTHCARE TO MANAGED CARE

In light of these findings one may ask, "How did we get to where we are today?" The answer has to do with the way the relationship between doctors and patients has evolved since World War II and also how US businesses became involved in supplying medical insurance to their employees.

For a good part of the twentieth century, the relationship between doctors and their patients was direct: Doctors serviced their patients often through home visits much like those portrayed in the television series *Marcus Welby, M.D.*[5] In return, doctors received fees for their services; consequently, this system was called "fee for service." Private sector health insurance began prior to the 1930s, but by the start of World War II only about 10 million Americans were covered. The broader expansion of healthcare coverage through corporations took off in the 1950s, as companies could pool risks and thereby lessen adverse selection. At the same time, employers were allowed to deduct premiums from paychecks, which reduced administrative costs.

As regards government involvement, there were several failed efforts to enact national health insurance in the first part of the twentieth century, and the federal government played a secondary role to the states. During the mid-1960s, the federal government became more proactive with Congressional passage of Medicare and Medicaid as part of the Great Society initiative.

While these programs helped to shrink the number of elderly and poor who did not receive any coverage, it soon became apparent that medical costs were advancing much more rapidly than overall inflation. One reason is they substantially increased the demand for US healthcare, as millions who previously lacked coverage acquired it. Second, as the government covered a larger portion of the healthcare bill, the share of out-of-pocket expenses decreased and that of third parties increased from 45% in 1960 to 67% in 1975.[6] (Note: The share of out-of-pocket expenses has since fallen to just over 10% of total costs.)

In response to this development, the federal government in 1973 passed the HMO Act that was designed to promote and encourage development of

---

[4] Ibid.

[5] This analogy is depicted in David Dranove's book, *Code Red: An Economist Explains How to Revive the Healthcare System without Destroying It*, Princeton University Press, 2008.

[6] See Stephanie Kelton, cFEPS, "An Introduction to the Health Care Crisis in America; How Did We Get Here?" September 2007.

HMOs.[7] One of the stated objectives was to give people a choice as to the type of healthcare delivery system they could use. A second objective was to reform the healthcare delivery system to bring about greater organizational efficiency together with more effective control of quality of care. A third objective was to provide cost control, including providing incentives for the delivery system and enabling federal and state programs to control healthcare expenditures with predictable prepaid contracts for beneficiaries.

As HMOs proliferated, people found themselves confronting the following issues: Should they continue to get healthcare in the traditional manner, seeing their own independent physician, pay a fee for each visit and file a claim with an insurance company? Or, should they sign up with a managed-care company that provides and manages all their medical care for a set monthly fee? And if they opted to switch, which kind of managed-care company (HMO, PPO among others) should they join?

Over time, businesses made managed-care programs part of the plans employees could select, and many opted to enroll in them because they were cheaper than the traditional fee for service model. For a while in the 1990s, it appeared that such programs were effective at containing costs. However, as HMOs switched their status from being nonprofit organizations to ones that were for-profit, increases in health insurance premiums far outstripped wage and price inflation beginning in the late 1990s and continuing into the following decade. Part of the reason is the premiums that were being charged included considerable profit margins and administrative costs.

Indeed, many physicians are critical of the switch to managed care, contending that it severed the direct link doctors had with their patients and also that purported cost savings reflected a lower quality of care. More broadly, patients and providers complained about problems with healthcare quality, which were documented in two studies by the Institutes of Medicine.[8]

In his book, *Your Money or Your Life*, David M. Cutler, a Harvard economist who served on President Clinton's healthcare task force, claims the majority of health analysts believe managed care is doing what it is supposed to do—namely, saving money without compromising health.[9] Yet he acknowledges how unpopular it is:

> It is hard to overstate how much people hate managed care. Public opinion surveys show that managed care is among the most disliked of all industries, with roughly the support of tobacco and oil and gas companies.[10]

[7] For a discussion of the goals of the legislation see B.A. Meyers, "Health Maintenance Organizations: Objectives and Issues," HSMHA Health Rep. July 1971, pp. 585–591.

[8] See Institutes of Medicine, "Too Err is Human: Building a Safer Health System," November 1999.

[9] David M. Cutler, *Your Money or Your Life*, Oxford University press, 2004.

[10] Ibid, p. 94.

Cutler attributes this to managed care telling people they have to cut back, and so it takes the blame.

Rejection of Universal Coverage

As indicated previously, the federal government took a backseat in addressing the issue of medical coverage until the mid-1960s, when the Johnson administration embarked on the Great Society. Two prior administrations—FDR's in the early 1930 and Harry Truman's after World War II—contemplated the need for universal healthcare coverage. However, Roosevelt ultimately decided against enacting legislation because of stiff opposition from the AMA and his concern that it could undermine passage of social security legislation.[11] Truman also backed away from the idea amid public concerns at the time about the threat of communism, and assertions that universal coverage was tantamount to socialized medicine.

The principal attempt to gain universal coverage occurred during the first term of the Clinton administration. Bill Clinton made healthcare reform a key component of his policy proposals during the 1992 presidential campaign, and upon assuming office he appointed Hillary Clinton to chair a task force to make policy recommendations. The main stipulation was that each US citizen and permanent resident must become enrolled in a qualified health plan on his/her own or through those mandated by businesses with more than 5000 full-time employees, while those too poor to afford coverage would be subsidized. The bill that was drafted by the task force was a complex proposal of more than 1000 pages, which included a host of stipulations including a list of mandatory benefits to be offered: Establishment of a National Health Board to oversee the quality of services, federal funding in case of insolvency of state programs, long-term care provisions, coverage for abortions and prescription drug benefit among others.

In a speech to a joint session of Congress on September 22, 1993, President Clinton explained the need to pass the Health Security Act in the following terms:

> Millions of Americans are just a pink slip away from losing their health insurance, and one serious illness away from losing their savings. Millions more are locked into jobs they have now just because they or someone in their family has once been sick and they have what is called the preexisting condition. And on any given day, over 37 million Americans – most of them working people and their little children – have no health insurance at all. And in spite of this, our medical bills are growing at over twice the rate of inflation, and the United States spends over a third more of its income on health care than any other nation on earth.[12]

---

[11] See Kelton, op. cit.
[12] Bill Clinton, Address to Joint Session of Congress, September 22, 1993.

The bill, however, encountered stiff opposition from Republicans and the health insurance industry, who sarcastically called it "Hillarycare." And even though the Democrats controlled both houses of Congress, they were not united in supporting the legislation, and several members offered plans of their own. A final compromise Democratic bill was declared dead on September 26, 1994. In the November mid-term elections that followed, the Republicans gained control of the House of Representatives partly in response to a voter backlash.

THE LAUNCH OF OBAMACARE

Healthcare insurance resurfaced as an important issue in the 2008 presidential election, when Barrack Obama and Hillary Clinton campaigned on making medical coverage affordable for Americans who were not covered by employers, government programs or themselves. Upon assuming office, President Obama made passage of healthcare legislation one of his top two priorities along with reform of the financial system.

The ACA that was enacted in 2010 contained several key provisions including the following: First, individuals without insurance were mandated to buy insurance or pay a penalty unless they faced a financial hardship or were members of a religious sect that exempted them. States were authorized to create exchanges where people could purchase insurance. Second, businesses that employed 50 or more people but which do not offer health insurance to full-time employees would pay a penalty if the government has subsidized healthcare through tax deductions. Third, a partial community rating requires insurers to offer the same premium to applicants of the same age and location without regard to gender or pre-existing conditions. Moreover, premiums for older applicants could be no more than three times those for the youngest. Fourth, eligibility for Medicaid was extended to families whose income was up to nearly 140% of the poverty line from 100% previously.

Each of these provisions ultimately became a bone of contention for Republicans who opposed the bill. However, the nature of the opposition changed from the time the bill was launched until present.

One of the first attacks on Obamacare was from conservative Republicans and libertarians who objected to the government mandating that people purchase insurance.

After it was passed, they challenged the concept in the courts on grounds it was unconstitutional, but the Supreme Court ultimately ruled against this interpretation.

The reason for including the individual mandate provision is common to any attempt to create an insurance pool—namely, absent any rules people opting to buy insurance are more likely to have high-risk factors, which is commonly known as adverse selection. If those who are healthy wait to join until they are at risk—known as the free rider problem—the insurance pool would be too small, and costs would skyrocket, which would make the pool unviable.[13] The intent of the individual mandate is to prevent this from happening.

Meanwhile, the tax legislation that was ultimately enacted at the end of 2017 included a provision that repealed the individual mandate, which President Trump declared effectively repealed Obamacare.

ATTEMPT TO REPEAL OBAMACARE

During the 2016 election campaign one of the rallying cries for Republicans was to repeal Obamacare and replace it with an alternative that was deemed to be superior. This time, the debate shifted away from the individual mandate provision to the contention that Obamacare was failing and therefore would need to be replaced.

The evidence that was marshaled in support of this position was that insurers were withdrawing participation from public exchanges in a growing number of states, and that in some instances only one provider was left. Furthermore, premiums had risen considerably during 2016—by 16% for the bellwether silver program—which would likely force more people to abandon their coverage. The response of Democrats was the system is fundamentally sound, but public worries about changes in the program's status under a Republican-controlled government had fueled instability. In their view, it is incumbent for the Republican leadership to make clear it will not allow the system to fail, especially considering the ACA has reduced the ranks of the uninsured by more than 20 million people.

A second line of Republican attack against Obamacare was that most of the increase in coverage was the result of expansion of Medicaid enrollees. This occurred because the ACA expanded eligibility for Medicaid to nearly 140% of the poverty line from 100% previously. One of the bones of contention of the Republican leadership was that Medicaid expansion represented an unfunded liability of the federal and state governments. Indeed, according to the CBO, it would add more than $1 trillion in expenses to the federal budget over the next ten years. The House Republicans, in turn, proposed that Medicaid expansion should be curtailed after a specified date, and that states would be awarded block grants to cover existing commitments.

However, when it came time for House Republicans to develop an alternative to Obamacare, they soon learned it is not easy to coalesce around a common plan. One of the most serious problems they encountered was that it was

---

[13] Ironically, the concept is linked to The Heritage Foundation, a conservative think tank, and to Republican senators who were seeking a market-based approach to healthcare reform in the early 1990s. In the wake of the Clinton administration's plan for universal coverage, the Republicans countered with an alternative, the Health Equity and Access Reform Today Act (HEART Act) that included an individual mandate provision. It was not until the Affordable Care Act was enacted that the Republicans challenged the individual mandate as being unconstitutional.

difficult to find ways to reduce expenses, which would enable premiums to be lowered, without compromising benefits that the electorate valued. Foremost among these was the provision that mandated insurance companies could not deny coverage due to pre-existing conditions. Similarly, House Republicans differed on when Medicaid expansion should be terminated and the degree of support.

While the House eventually was able to pass a bill, its prospects in the Senate were far from clear, and the Senate began from scratch in drafting its own bill. One reason: The House bill was unpopular with the electorate at large, and according to CBO, its passage would result in more than 20 million Americans dropping their coverage. Ultimately, Senate Republicans were unable to reach agreement on a bill; consequently, much to the chagrin of President Trump and the Republican leadership, the ACA remained the law of the land.

A National Dilemma: What Can Be Done to Control Medical Costs?

While many are quick to blame the Republicans for putting the lives of many Americans at risk if they cannot afford coverage, there is no denying that medical costs have been rising at an unacceptable pace since entitlement programs took off in the mid-1960s. Indeed, medical costs cumulatively have increased more than three times faster than wages and core inflation (see Fig. 4.1).

This is a critical issue for the electorate, as the United States now spends more than 17% of GDP on healthcare, in the vicinity twice that of other advanced countries, and it is projected to rise steadily into the future. (By comparison, the US healthcare spend was 5% of GDP in the 1960s.) While many Americans are leading longer and better lives as a result of medical advances, the same is true of other countries, who collectively pay far less for comparable outcomes.

One of the disappointments is that previous efforts to reform the US system have not altered the situation. The creation of managed care, for example, was heralded as a way to rationalize the system and lower costs; yet, this failed to materialize, partly because of built-in expenses for administration and profit margins. Also, many physicians and patients complain that the attempts by providers to negotiate lower prices for services wound up sacrificing quality of coverage.

Similarly, part of the rationale for adopting universal coverage during the Clinton administration was the single-payer model would help reduce administration costs while also increasing the government's bargaining power with pharmaceutical companies. However, for reasons cited it was not implemented.

As discussed in Chap. 3, the major challenge the government faces in the years ahead is the need to finance rapid growth of entitlement programs as the number of baby boomers retire. In this regard, Obamacare has added to the

Fig. 4.1 Medical inflation far exceeds core inflation and wage inflation, 1965–2017. (Source: US Bureau of Labor Statistics)

burden, because by expanding eligibility for Medicaid the federal government has effectively assumed an unfunded liability of more than $1 trillion over the next ten years. While the Republican leadership in Congress is trying to reduce this commitment, it cannot come clean with the electorate for fear that voters would object. The challenge, therefore, is how to initiate a dialogue so the electorate can make an informed decision.

In this regard, columnist Robert J. Samuelson points out that the consequences of doing nothing are that more and more government programs are skewed to the elderly rather than to the youth of our country.[14] He notes that although three-quarters of Medicaid recipients are either children or young adults, they account for only one-third of the costs. The elderly and disabled constitute one-quarter of the recipients but represent two-thirds of the costs. Samuelson goes on to point out that much of the latter goes to pay for nursing homes and other long-term care, and that the tally will surge as the population ages, both due to increased numbers of people and also because costs rise as the elderly require more care. This situation is putting added burdens on state governments, which share expenses with the federal government, and it is usurping priorities such as schools and other state programs.

Samuelson believes the solution would be to transfer Medicaid's long-term care to the federal government, merging it with Medicare. In return, the states would assume all Medicaid costs for children and younger adults. While the proposal would help put Medicaid on more sound footings, Samuelson is not optimistic about anything happening politically:

[14] See Robert J. Samuelson, "How to Get Medicaid under Control," *The Washington Post*, March 20, 2017.

Unfortunately, there is little support for this sort of swap. Commentators (including this reporter) periodically propose it and praise its benefits. But national politicians seem uninterested. They prefer instead to bleed the states.[15]

SUMMARY: NO EASY FIX

The American healthcare system is like no other, an amalgam in which insurance coverage is provided by employers, individuals and the government at the federal and state levels. Unlike most advanced countries, there is no universal coverage, and prior to the passage of the ACA more than 40 million Americans had no coverage.

Since the mid-1960s the long-standing goal of the Democratic Party has been to increase the federal government's involvement in healthcare and to reduce the number of people without coverage. Republicans were originally opposed to this on philosophical grounds, arguing that "socialized medicine" would undermine the quality of care and lessen the supply of physicians.

Over time, as more people were covered by government programs, the stance of the Republican Party shifted. During the Clinton administration, when universal healthcare was being proposed, the Republicans favored the idea of private exchanges. When this concept became an integral part of the ACA, however, the Republican leadership objected to restrictions and taxes that it contained, and they argued that the system of exchanges was failing.

Now that the Republicans control both the White House and Congress they are discovering how difficult it is to find an alternative that is acceptable to the various segments of the party. Specifically, the far right favors repeal of Obamacare, whereas moderates wish to retain certain features including the right to have affordable insurance for pre-existing conditions.

It would be a mistake, however, to conclude that the inability to achieve viable healthcare reform is purely the result of political differences. In his book *Code Red*, David Danove acknowledges the insight of Columbia University's policy guru, Eli Ginzberg, who observed the healthcare industry has too many power centers, including physicians, hospitals, insurers, pharmaceutical companies and employers. Based on this consideration Danove concludes:

> It seems that no one has offered a health reform proposal that does not adversely affect at least two power centers. Insurers and suppliers oppose proposals that rely on significant expansion of government powers, while providers and patient advocates have shown little interest in market-based solutions, especially if they promote managed care. The result is perpetual legislative gridlock.[16]

---

[15] Ibid.
[16] Danove, op. cit., p. 5.

David Culter also believes the failure to achieve fundamental reform stems from more than pure political differences, but he offers a more basic explanation:

> It is great that more people will be covered by health care reform, but who will volunteer to sacrifice their own care to achieve this? ...People with insurance fear that their care will be worse so that others can have insurance coverage. It is not a winning strategy.[17]

Faced with this reality, people need to recognize there are no "magic bullets" to cure the US healthcare system. The relevant issue, instead, is in which direction is the system headed. In this regard, the trend appears to be toward greater government involvement to cover basic needs through an expansion of Medicare, with private insurers covering supplemental needs. (Note: At the end of this chapter we consider whether healthcare is compatible with free markets, as some prominent economists have pondered, and cite the counter-argument as well.)

However, as discussed in Chap. 3, Americans will ultimately have to decide who pays for the government programs, as financing them through increased federal borrowing is becoming increasingly untenable. This, in turn, raises the issue of whether America can afford sweeping tax cuts for individuals and families, a topic that is covered in the next chapter.

INVESTMENT IMPLICATIONS FOR THE HEALTHCARE SECTOR

While the debate over the repeal and replacement of Obamacare has grabbed the headlines in political commentaries, one of the surprises is that it has largely been a nonevent for the US stock market: As shown in Fig. 4.2, healthcare stocks have performed roughly in line with the broad market as a whole (see lower panel). This outcome is considerably different from what transpired during the debate over universal coverage in 1993 and early 1994, when the healthcare sector underperformed the broad market by as much as 25% until the legislation was defeated, and healthcare stocks subsequently recovered. Similarly, during the debate over the ACA in 2010, the healthcare sector underperformed the broad market by as much as 15%, before recovering in 2012.

This begs the question: Why have equity investors seemingly been unexcited by the prospect of repealing and replacing Obamacare? I believe there are two possibilities. One is that investors are not sure what the ultimate outcome will be and therefore are staying on the sidelines. The other possibility is investors view changes in legislation as impacting only a small segment of the healthcare sector—namely, insurance companies whose business models are aimed at serving

[17] Cutler, op. cit., p. 122.

Fig. 4.2 Healthcare sector vs. S&P 500, relative return (in %)

Medicaid patients or those on exchanges. By comparison, pharmaceutical companies, hospitals and insurance companies that served the broader market were likely to be adversely impacted to a much greater extent by "Hillarycare," which provoked a much greater market response.

Is HealthCare Compatible with Free Markets?

Amid the challenges Republicans have encountered in finding an alternative to Obamacare, some observers have questioned whether healthcare is compatible with a market-based system. This debate goes back to the early 1960s, when the Ford Foundation approached Kenneth Arrow, a Stanford University economist who went on to become a Nobel laureate, to investigate the issue. Arrow subsequently published a paper titled "Uncertainty and the Welfare Economics of Medical Care" that is considered the seminal piece on the subject.[18]

Arrow's principal finding is that a "laissez-faire solution for medicine is intolerable, that the delivery system of health care deviates from a classical free market, and therefore, that the government must intervene to correct these distortions."[19] He identified five key distinctions in the market for healthcare services and products: (i) Unpredictability about when and whether people will need healthcare services, (ii) barriers to entry in the form of extensive medical training that limit the supply of physicians, (iii) the importance of trust between doctors and patients, (iv) asymmetrical information in which doctors know much more about medicine than their patients and (v) Idiosyncratic payment of medical services, in which the patient is billed after the services are rendered.

Of these factors, Paul Krugman argues there are two strongly distinctive aspects of healthcare that differentiate it from other products and services.[20] One is that if you do need insurance, someone other than the patients ends up making decisions about what to buy: "Consumer choice is nonsense when it comes to health care. And you can't trust insurance companies either—they're not in business for their health, or yours."[21] The second key difference is that in deciding on medical services you can't rely on experience of comparison shopping, which is why doctors are supposed to follow an ethical code. Krugman concludes that these factors do not mean that socialized medicine or single-payer model is the only way to go, but that there are a number of successful healthcare systems, as measured by quality of care and cost effectiveness, than in the United States.

The response from conservatives is that the most noteworthy advantages of a market-oriented system include the following: First, consumers

(*continued*)

---

[18] Kenneth Arrow, *American Economic Review*, Vol. 53, Issue 5, (Dec. 1963).

[19] See Megan McCardle, "Liberals Are Wrong: Free Market Health Care is Possible," theatalantic.com, March 18, 2012.

[20] See Paul Krugman's blog, "Why markets can't cure healthcare," July 2, 2009.

[21] Ibid.

(continued)

should benefit from having choices among providers (even if they are not always easy ones to make). Second, competition among providers should help drive down premiums on policies (as well as force insurers to look after their customers' interests). Third, they tend to be more innovative than government-mandated systems due to competitive pressures.

A possible solution that David Dranove and Craig Carthwaite of Northwestern University put forth is the notion of modifying Obamacare so it is more flexible than the current arrangement.[22] They contend that if the ACA is distilled to its most basic components, the most important feature is its introduction of competition in private health insurance through the creation exchanges, which at the core is a Republican idea. In their view, the problem with Obamacare is that it is burdened by too many regulations that hamper competition, and they propose the following modifications: First, repeal the employer mandate so that businesses no longer are obligated to provide health insurance to employees. Second, scale back the minimum benefit package, which would allow insurers to innovate on the design of benefit packages. Third, repeal the prohibition on catastrophic health plans, and allow individuals who purchase high deductible plans to receive the same subsidy as those purchasing plans for the "silver" tier of the exchange. Fourth, level the tax playing field, such that employer-sponsored insurance is not favored over insurance purchased privately on the exchanges.

The main point of Dranove-Carthwaite analysis is that it is possible to utilize private exchanges to provide benefits from increased competition, but politicians on both sides of the aisle need to agree on a sensible list of regulations for them.

---

[22] See David Danove and Graig Garthwaite, "Here's A Republican Response to Obama's Call for Ideas to Reform the Health Care System," Business Insider, February 4, 2014.

CHAPTER 5

Tax Policy: Tax Cuts Versus Tax Reform

One issue that investors immediately latched on to following the 2016 elections was the prospect that the Trump administration and Republican-controlled Congress would enact significant corporate and personal income tax cuts. The stock market's initial surge, to a large extent, reflected investors' perceptions that tax cuts would help to boost the economy and corporate profits. Yet, while the link between tax cuts and economic growth is commonly accepted by most people, there have been few studies by economists that have investigated the relationship systematically. This chapter, therefore, begins by reviewing evidence about the impact of tax cuts on the US economic growth and tax revenues.

We next consider the difference between tax reform, which seeks to broaden the tax base by eliminating deductions and exclusions, and tax cuts that are intended to stimulate the economy. This distinction is particularly important in the current context in which the House Republican leadership drafted a bill in mid-2016 that was intended to be neutral with respect to the budget deficit, whereas the initial proposal put forth by the Trump administration would increase the federal deficit considerably. This posed a challenge for investors as they tried to anticipate what type of legislation would be enacted and the impact it would have on the economy.

The chapter also examines the case for cuts in corporate income taxes and for personal income taxes separately. The main argument for lowering corporate tax rates is they are well above the average of other advanced economies, which creates incentives for the US businesses to shift production abroad. This is one area where the goals of the Trump administration overlap with the Obama administration, but where the approach to resolve the issue is very different. By comparison, the case for steep cuts in personal income tax rate is less compelling, as tax rates in the United States are in line with other countries, and the economy is close to full employment.

The final issue that we consider is how the Tax Cuts and Jobs Act bill that was passed in December will impact the economy and financial markets. Equity investors continue to believe significant tax cuts will boost corporate profits and the economy, and they were a factor bolstering the stock market. A factor bolstering the stock market. Bond investors, however, are more concerned with the way tax cuts will be financed and the extent to which they will add to the budget deficit.

PERSPECTIVE ON US TAX CUTS

The stock market's favorable response to prospective tax cuts is self-evident for many people: It is widely perceived that cuts in corporate tax rates will boost after-tax profit margins for businesses, which in turn will boost after-tax earnings. At the same time, cuts in personal income tax rates are generally seen as boosting aggregate demand, which helps to spur overall profit growth. Accordingly, market participants believe the combination of corporate and personal tax cuts will boost economic growth and profit growth simultaneously.

The challenge that economists face in examining this relationship is there are relatively few experiences of significant US tax cuts in the post-war period. Therefore, we begin by considering the most important tax cuts.

Kennedy Tax Cut

The first was tax cuts proposed by President Kennedy in 1962 that were enacted by Congress in early 1964, three months after his assassination. In a speech to the Economic Club of New York in 1962, Kennedy indicated he was committed to "an across-the-board, top-to-bottom cut in personal and corporate income taxes" that were designed to boost the economy.[1] The top marginal rate for personal income taxes at the time was 91%, which JFK was seeking to lower to 65%. Kennedy contended the tax system that was designed during World War II "exerts too heavy a drag on growth in peace time; that it siphons out of the private economy too large a share of personal and business purchasing power; that it reduces the financial incentives for personal effort, investment and risk-taking."

The bill that was ultimately passed was the Revenue Act of 1964 and was commonly known as the Tax Reduction Act. It reduced the top marginal tax rate for individuals to 70% and created a minimum standard deduction, while it lowered the corporate tax rate from 52% to 48%. Democrats supported the bill on grounds that the biggest tax cuts were aimed at average workers, who would use the tax savings to increase spending. Indeed, it marked the first time that tax cuts were enacted in peace time when the economy was not weak, and in this respect it was widely considered to be a form of Keynesian stimulus.[2] By and large, the experience is considered to have been a success, as economic growth accelerated in the mid-1960s while tax revenues also increased.

---

[1] Marilyn Geewax, "JFK's Lasting Economic Legacy: Lower Tax Rates," NPR special series, November 14, 2013.
[2] Robert Schlesinger, "The Myth of JFK as Supply Side Tax Cutter," US News and World Report, January 26, 2011.

Reagan Tax Cut

Although Congressional Republicans supported the final bill that was enacted, the majority of Republicans balked at passing the initial legislation in 1963 on grounds that it would create large budget deficits. This remained a traditional concern of the GOP until Ronald Reagan was elected President in November 1980, when the party's emphasis switched from containing budget deficits to restoring economic growth.

Reagan's 1981 Program for Economic Recovery had four major policy objectives: (i) Reduce the growth of government spending, (ii) lower marginal tax rates on income for both labor and capital, (iii) diminish government regulation and (iv) reduce inflation by controlling the growth of money supply. The crux of Reaganomics was a belief in "supply-side" economics, which held that economic agents—households and businesses—would respond significantly to reductions in marginal tax rates and government regulations.

Leading supply-side proponents such as Jack Kemp, Art Laffer and Jude Waniski embraced the JFK tax cuts as embodying the principles they articulated. They popularized the idea that cuts in tax rates could actually boost tax revenues with a parabola that Art Laffer reportedly sketched (Fig. 5.1). It showed there was a tax rate level beyond which government revenues would decline because people would be discouraged to work more hours.

The Economic Recovery Tax Act of 1981 was enacted "to encourage economic growth through reductions in individual income tax rates, the expensing of depreciable property, incentives for small businesses, and incentives for savings, and for other purposes." The key provisions included an across-the-board decrease in income tax rates of 23%, with the top rate falling from 70% to 50%, indexation of tax rates to inflation, accelerated depreciation allowances for businesses and creation of individual retirement accounts (IRAs).

Although Republicans hailed the Reagan tax cuts as contributing to the economic recovery and expansion that began in mid-1982, they have been the subject of considerable controversy. The main reason is they were also associated with significant increases in federal budget deficits in the 1980s: The federal budget deficit rose from 2.6% of GDP in 1981 to 5–6% of GDP from 1983 to 1986. This is partly attributable to President Reagan seeking to expand military spending and the instance of Democrats that this be combined with expanded funding for social programs. Beyond this, claims by supply-siders

Fig. 5.1 The Laffer curve: linking government revenues to marginal tax rates

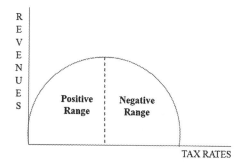

that tax cuts would be self-financing proved to be overly optimistic. OMB Budget Director David Stockman even conceded that the administration's projections were based on a "rosy scenario" in which rapid growth would generate sufficient revenues to pay for the tax cuts.

Reagan Tax Reforms

In order to address the budget deficit problem and concerns about the viability of the social security system, President Reagan subsequently signed off on several bills to boost government revenues. They did so largely by broadening the tax base—that is, by reducing various federal tax breaks and closing tax loopholes—rather than by raising marginal tax rates. In 1983 President Reagan also signed off on Social Security reform legislation that sought to maintain its viability by accelerating an increase in the payroll tax rate among other changes.

Three years later Congress passed The Tax Reform Act of 1986 that was designed to simplify the income tax code, broaden the tax base and eliminate many tax shelters. The bill received impetus from the US Treasury, which designed it to be revenue neutral in accordance with the President's stance that he would veto any bill that was not. Eugene Steuerle, who served as a deputy assistant Treasury secretary at the time, observed:

> What people forget about Ronald Reagan was that he was very much converted to base broadening as a means of reducing deficits and as a means of tax reform.[3]

Looking back on the historic legislation 20 years later, *Washington Post* columnist Jeffrey H. Birnbaum noted both its accomplishments and challenges as follows[4]:

> The Tax Reform Act of 1986 – the biggest and most controversial legislative story of its time – had lawmakers, lobbyists and journalists in Washington in an uproar for two years. Despite nearly dying several times, the measure eventually passed, producing a simpler code with fewer tax breaks and significantly lower rates. These changes affected every family and business in the nation.
>
> In the years since, however, rates have gradually risen and Congress has passed nearly 15,000 changes to the tax law. Many of the loopholes that disappeared two decades ago are back.

In reviewing changes in tax policy during the Reagan years what stands out is that the highest marginal tax rates were lowered from 70% to 28% while tax rates were indexed to inflation for the first time. These changes along with a significant easing in monetary policy discussed in Chap. 7 contributed to an economic revival beginning in mid-1982. The tax rate cuts, however, were

[3] Jeanne Sahadi, "Taxes: What people forgot about Reagan," CNN Money, September 12, 2010.
[4] Andrew Chamberlain, "Twenty Years Later: The Tax Reform Act of 1986," Tax Foundation, October 22, 2006.

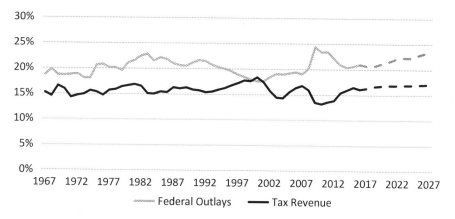

30%
25%
20%
15%
10%
5%
0%

1967 1972 1977 1982 1987 1992 1997 2002 2007 2012 2017 2022 2027

·········· Federal Outlays   ▬▬ Tax Revenue

Fig. 5.2 Federal government spending and revenues (% of GDP). (Note: Figures for 2017–2027 are forecasts. Source: Congressional Budget Office)
Tax Revenue includes Individual Income Taxes, Payroll Taxes, and Corporate Income Taxes

not self-financing, and ultimately the tax base had to be broadened to bring the budget deficit under control. Over the full two terms of the Reagan administration, tax revenues as a percent of GDP matched the average in the four prior decades, while federal government spending was higher—22.4% of GDP versus 20.7% (see Fig. 5.2).

Impact of Tax Cuts/Reform on Growth

As noted previously, there are few studies that have examined the link between tax rate changes and economic growth in depth. The most comprehensive is a paper by William G. Gale and Andrew A. Samwick titled "Effects of Income Tax Changes on Economic Growth."[5] The study focused on two types of tax changes—reductions in individual tax rates and income tax reform that broadens the tax base while lowering tax rates. Following are some of their principal findings:

- While tax policy can influence economic choices, it is not obvious that tax rate cuts will ultimately lead to a larger economy in the long run. The reason: While they raise the after-tax return to working, saving and investing, they also raise after-tax incomes, which lessen the need to work, save and invest.
- The historical evidence and simulation analyses suggest that tax rate cuts that are financed by debt for an extended period will have little positive impact on long-term growth and could reduce growth.

[5]William G. Gale and Andrew A. Samwick, "Effects of Income Tax Changes on Economic Growth," Brookings Institution and Tax Policy Center, February 2016.

- Tax reform is more complex, as it involves tax rate cuts as well as base-broadening changes. One advantage of base broadening is reallocating resources from sectors that are tax-preferred to ones that have the highest (pre-tax) return, which would increase overall economic efficiency.

The paper concludes by observing that not all tax changes will have the same impact on growth: "Reforms that improve incentives, reduce existing distortionary subsidies, avoid windfall gains, and avoid deficit financing will have more auspicious effects on the long-term size of the economy, but may also create trade-offs between equity and efficiency."[6]

The above findings are relevant in the current context in which there are significant differences between the program of tax cuts that the Trump administration is considering and the tax reform legislation that the Republican House leadership drafted in mid-2016.

The Republican-sponsored House bill was intended to be deficit neutral. It would offset the effects of personal and corporate tax rate cuts by eliminating many personal deductions and business deductions for interest payments. By comparison, the tax plan that Donald Trump submitted during the 2016 presidential campaign contained few items to broaden the tax base, and the assessment of several independent research organizations was that it would significantly increase the budget deficit over the next ten years. A subsequent proposal that was submitted by the OMB in April 2017 was closer to the House bill in that it would eliminate all itemized deductions except for the charities and mortgage interest payments. However, many commentators viewed the OMB submission as a "wish list" rather than a formal plan. Consequently, investors continued to focus on the House bill and possible modifications to it.

THE CASE FOR CORPORATE TAX CUTS

While both the draft House bill and the Trump administration's tax submission apply both to personal and corporate taxes, investors are paying the greatest attention to changes in the corporate tax rate, as it will have the most direct impact on corporate profits.

The case for revamping the corporate tax code is compelling for a variety of reasons. A recent study by Eric Toder and Alan D. Viard titled "A Proposal to Reform the Taxation of Corporate Income" contends the US corporate tax system is broken and outdated, because it has failed to adapt to several major developments.[7] They include the increased globalization of economic activity and the failure of the US tax system to keep pace with reductions in corporate tax rates in other major industrial countries and their shifts to territorial tax systems such as value-added taxes (VAT): The marginal tax rate in the United States of 39% (including a federal tax rate of 35% and effective state taxes of 4%) is the highest

---

[6] Ibid.

[7] Eric Toder and Alan D. Viard, "A Proposal to Reform the Taxation of Corporate Income," Tax Policy Center, Urban Institute and Brookings Institution, June 2016.

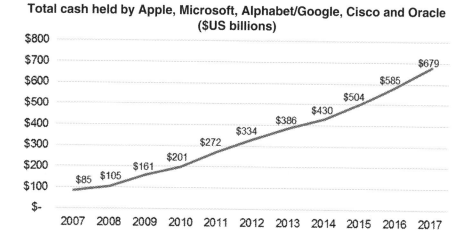

Total cash held by Apple, Microsoft, Alphabet/Google, Cisco and Oracle ($US billions)

Fig. 5.3   Cumulative cash of top 5 holders. (Source: Moody's)

among industrial countries. The objective of both the Trump administration and Congressional Republicans, therefore, is to lower the US corporate rate near 20%, which would bring it more in line with other countries.

A second type of distortion is the current system penalizes companies with predominantly domestic operations relative to those who have overseas affiliates. The reason is that multinationals can evade the higher US corporate tax rate by booking more of their profits abroad. According to IRS data, for example, the largest US businesses (annual revenues above $100 million) paid an average federal rate of about 23% on their taxable income in 2013 (the latest available data), compared with 32% for companies with sales between $10 million and $100 million and 27.5% for those with sales of less than $10 million.[8]

The challenge the United States faces is trying to harmonize tax rates with those of other countries. By allowing US-based multinationals to defer tax on most profits until they are repatriated, the United States effectively taxes foreign-source income at a much lower effective rate than domestic-source income. This method of taxation has caused the US multinationals to accumulate substantial profits held in low-tax jurisdictions abroad that are estimated to be between $2 trillion and $3 trillion. According to Moody's, US nonfinancial companies' cash and liquid investments reached $1.9 trillion at the end of 2017, of which the top five cash holders—Apple, Microsoft, Alphabet, Cisco and Oracle—are estimated at $679 billion, or roughly one-third of the total (Fig. 5.3).

This has been a contentious political issue in recent years. The Obama administration sought to establish rules to deal with so-called inversions—the practices of relocating a corporation's legal domicile to a lower-tax nation, or tax haven, while retaining its primary operations in its higher-tax country of origin. As Toder and Viard argue, however, it is very difficult to close tax loopholes in a world of today:

[8] See Martin H. Barnes, "U.S. Fiscal Policy: Facts, Fallacies and Fantasies," BCA Research, April 5, 2017.

The source of profits was more meaningful when most business wealth was in fixed assets, such as plant and equipment, whose location was easily defined. Today, however, a substantial share of business wealth is in intangible assets that are not location specific, such as patents, goodwill, business reputation, and corporate governance…In theory, the United States could tax the value of intangible assets when their ownership is initially transferred to a foreign affiliate, but it is often very difficult to value intangible assets at time of transfer, when their contribution to future profitability is not yet known.[9]

The Republican response is to create incentives for multinationals to repatriate profits by offering a one-time lower tax rate in the vicinity of 10% on average, and to eliminate tax distortions that favor overseas production relative to domestic production. The House Republican tax bill that was drafted, for example, included a BAT provision that is intended to make companies indifferent between paying taxes on domestic and foreign profits. It does so by excluding revenues on goods that are exported from the United States, which provides an effective subsidy to exports, while excluding the cost of imports as a deduction in computing net income, which effectively taxes them. Nonetheless, while proponents contend the BAT eliminates distortions in the tax code between foreign and domestic income, it is highly controversial, because it would adversely impact companies that have built their business models around creating global supply chains. Republican Congressional leaders were hoping to retain the provision in a modified form, as it is expected to generate more than $1 trillion in tax revenues over the next ten years, but it ultimately proved to be nonviable for political reasons.

Beyond the issue of tax harmonization, there is another long-standing problem of the corporate tax system that the Republican House tax bill seeks to address—namely, the current corporate income tax penalizes equity-financed investment relative to debt-financed corporate investment and investment by flow-through businesses. The reason: The latter types of investments are taxed only at the individual level while equity-financed corporate investment is taxed at both the corporate and individual levels and therefore faces a higher-tax burden.[10] The House Republican bill attempts to deal with this issue is by allowing companies to take full deductions on their investments immediately, while removing the tax deduction on their interest payments. The intent is to spur business capital spending without distorting how it is financed.

Many of the ideas were subsequently incorporated into the so-called Big 6 Tax Framework that was drafted in late September 2017. It represented the initial attempt to coalesce the views of the Congressional Republican leadership with those of White House.[11] The Framework, for example, set a corporate tax

[9]Toder and Viard, op. cit., p. 9.

[10]The paper also notes that the current system penalizes corporations that pay dividends because shareholders are taxed on dividends, relative to corporations that reinvest corporate earnings.

[11]The name refers to the six leaders involved in drafting the proposal: Paul Ryan, Mitch McConnell, Orrin Hatch and Kevin Brady representing Congressional Republicans, and Steve Mnuchin and Gary Cohn representing the White House.

rate of 20% and a 25% rate for pass-through businesses, granted five years of bonus depreciation, placed a limit on interest expense deduction and moved toward a territorial tax system in which businesses are taxed only on local income and not from income earned abroad.

Proposed Personal Tax Cuts

By comparison, the initial proposal put forth by the Trump administration to reduce personal taxes received little attention from investors. The main reason is it was more of a sketch—a one-page submission—rather than a concrete plan. The proposal would reduce the number of tax rates from seven brackets to three, while cutting the top rate from 39.6% to 35% and setting the other two brackets at 25% and 10% (since revised to 12%). However, it did not specify the incomes that would apply to each level; consequently, it was not possible to calculate precisely what the changes would mean in dollars and cents for individual tax payers. The proposal also called for repealing the Alternative Minimum tax, the estate tax and the 3.8% Medicare surtax that applies to wages and investments above certain thresholds.

To help finance the cuts, the proposal would eliminate all deductions except those for mortgage interest payments and charitable contributions. The most important is elimination of the deduction for state and local taxes (SALT), which is projected to boost federal revenues by $1 trillion over ten years. Considering how controversial many of these items are, the inclination of many investors was to wait until a joint House-Senate bill was drafted before reacting.

Democrats were quick to criticize the Trump administration's proposal as a "reverse Robin Hood" agenda that would benefit the very wealthy but do relatively little for the poor and middle class. They have argued that so-called trickle-down theory does not work in practice (see accompanying note on page 69 and Fig. 5.4).

Survey data by the Pew Research Center suggests there is a fairly wide divide on the issue of fairness by taxpayers.[12] For example, in 2014 (the latest data available from the IRS) people with adjusted gross income above $250,000 paid over half (51.6%) of all individual income taxes, while accounting for less than 3% of all returns filed (Table 5.1).[13] The Pew Center survey revealed that 54% of the respondents said they paid about the right amount of taxes for what they were getting from the federal government versus 40% who said they pay more than their fair share. In a separate survey taken in 2015, however, six in ten Americans surveyed said they were bothered by the feeling that "some wealthy people" and "some corporations" don't pay their fair share.

---

[12] Drew Desilver, "High-income Americans pay most income taxes, but enough to be fair/," Pew Research Center, April 13, 2016.
[13] Ibid.

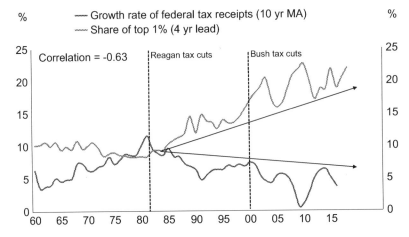

Fig. 5.4   Have tax cuts increased inequality? (Source: BLS, FRED, Piketty 2014 database, DB Global Markets Research)

Table 5.1   Distribution of tax payments by income brackets, 2014

Individual income tax statistics, by income group

Adjusted gross income	% of returns filed	% of income tax paid
Less than $15,000	24.3	0.1
$15,000–$29,999	20.4	1.4
$30,000–$49,000	17.6	4.1
$50,000–$99,000	21.7	14.9
$100,000–$199,99	11.8	21.9
$200,000–$249,999	1.5	5.9
$250,000 and above	2.7	51.6

Source: Internal Revenue Service, Pew Research Center

Beyond the issue of fairness, there are other factors to be considered in deciding whether personal income tax cuts represent good public policy at this time. The goal of the Trump administration is to boost growth, and it views tax cuts as a means to achieve its goal. However, many economists question the timing. With the economic expansion nearly a decade old and unemployment close to a record low, for example, one concern is that fiscal stimulus could cause the economy to overheat and potentially abort it.

Finally, another issue to be considered is where the economy is operating today along the Laffer curve. At the time of the Kennedy and Reagan tax cuts, the marginal tax rates for individuals were 90% and 70%, respectively. Today, by comparison they are below 40%. Consequently, the associated impact on the economy is likely to be considerably smaller.

Does "Trickle-Down" Economics Really Work?

Since the Reagan administration implemented tax cuts for individuals and businesses in 1981, there has been an ongoing debate between Republicans and Democrats about whether they benefit the average worker. Republicans have argued that insofar as tax cuts boost overall economic growth they will ultimately raise incomes for workers as well. This concept came to be known as "trickle-down theory."

In a book titled *Unequal Democracy* by Larry Bartels, a leading political scientist, the author challenges the empirical underpinnings of this argument.[14] One of the main findings of the book is that there has been a significant difference between the income gap between rich and poor since the mid-1970s. While Bartels acknowledges factors such as globalization, technological change and demographic shifts have contributed to this development, he contends that growing income inequality is also a political phenomenon.

Specifically, Bartels links some of the increased income inequality to the predilection of Republican administrations to favor tax cuts that favor the wealthy while Democrat administrations cater to the middle class and the poor. For example, Bartels observes that the income gap increased under presidents Eisenhower, Nixon, Ford, Reagan and both Bushes, while it declined under four of the five Democrat presidents (Carter being the exception) who served up to 2008, when the book was written. According to Bartels, the pattern "seems hard to attribute to a mere coincidence in the timing of Democratic and Republican administrations."

Another finding is that from 1948 to 2005 income growth for all income levels was better under Democratic presidents than Republican presidents. This calculation, however, may be influenced by lags when presidents assumed office. For example, President Reagan's administration began when inflation was rampant and monetary policy was being tightened considerably, which set the stage for a severe recession in 1982. Similarly, George W. Bush assumed office just as the tech bubble burst and one year later 9/11 occurred. Therefore, one needs to be careful in linking cause and effect.

Note: In Chap. 9 of this book, we examine the issue of inequality in more depth and, in particular, the role that globalization and educational attainment play in contributing to it not only in the United States but around the world.

PERSPECTIVE ON THE TAX CUTS AND JOBS ACT

One of the biggest questions for investors at the start of 2017 was whether major tax legislation would be enacted and, if so, how effective it would be in boosting economic growth in the near term and long term. In the wake of the

[14]Larry Bartels, *Unequal Democracy: The Political Economy of the New Gilded Age*, Princeton University, 2008.

fiasco over healthcare reform, the prevailing view was that Congressional Republicans were under intense pressure to pass tax legislation. Otherwise, they would head into the 2018 midterm elections with nothing to show for their efforts.

The outlines of a plan were spelled out in a House Republican tax proposal that was unveiled in early November. The plan, named "The Tax Cuts and Jobs Act," incorporated several provisions of "The Big 6 Tax Framework" that was agreed to by Republican leaders from the White House, House of Representatives and Senate. They included lower tax rates for corporations and pass-through businesses and for individuals. The plan also adopted the blueprint agreed upon by Senate Republicans to limit the increase in the budget deficit over the next ten years to $1 trillion, of which roughly two-thirds would apply to corporations and one-third to individuals.

Passage of House tax reform legislation in mid-November followed by a Senate tax reform bill in early December paved the way for a joint House-Senate conference to reconcile differences and agree on a unified bill that the full Senate and House needed to approve by simple majorities. Once this occurred President Trump immediately signed the bill, so the White House and GOP could claim they delivered on their signature legislation within the first year of their term.

The centerpiece of the legislation is changes to the corporate tax code that included the following provisions:

- *Corporate tax cuts*. Both the House and Senate versions proposed a permanent reduction in the marginal tax rate to 20% from 35%. However, the bill that was enacted set the rate at 21% to lessen the budgetary impact.
- *Pass Throughs*. The House proposed a 25% top tax rate, while the Senate allowed individuals to deduct 23% of domestic qualified business income. The final bill created a 20% deduction.
- *Expensing*. The law allows full expensing of short-lived capital investments for five years, and phases the change out thereafter.
- *Interest Deductibility*. The bill caps interest deductions at 30% of EBITDA for four years and 30% of EBIT after four years.
- *One-time tax on accumulated foreign profits*. The law enacts a deemed repatriation of overseas profits of 15.5% for cash and 8% for reinvested earnings.
- *International income*. The law introduces a territorial tax system for corporate international income, where US companies will not pay taxes on their overseas operations. Companies with over $500 million in annual gross receipts are subject to a tax—called the base erosion anti-abuse tax (BEAT)—that is designed to counter shifting of profits from one country to another with low or no taxes.

Some of the more controversial aspects of the legislation relate to tax treatment for individuals. For example, the bill repeals the individual mandate of the ACA that critics contend will weaken it. The House version would have eliminated the student-loan interest deduction, while the final bill preserves it. Both the Senate and House versions eliminated the state income and local sales tax deductions and capped property tax deductions at $10,000. The final bill capped SALT at $10,000 through 2025.

The legislation promises to be highly political, as it was passed without any Democratic support. Former Senator Judd Gregg, who was chairman of the Budget Committee and a member of the Simpson-Bowles Commission, offered the following assessment:

> Republicans are going to find that Democrats treat this tax bill the way Republicans treated Obamacare—it's not trusted by people on the other side of the aisle.... It will become a target, a rallying cry, which is unfortunate, because good tax reform, when done right, is not only good for the economy, it's good for both parties.[15]

One of the criticisms levied by Democrats is it favors the wealthy, who stand to gain from the expansion of the estate tax to $11 million per person, the amelioration of the alternative minimum tax and the favorable impact of corporate tax cuts on stock prices. President Trump and Congressional Republicans contend it benefits the middle class by nearly doubling the standard deduction for individual taxpayers and increasing the child tax credit, as well as by boosting wages as the economy expands.

Impact on Corporate Profits and Economic Growth

For equity investors the key issues are the impact that tax cuts and incentives will have on corporate profits, business investment and long-term economic growth. To a large extent, the surge in the stock market in late 2017 reflected the impact they will have in boosting after-tax corporate profits. Goldman Sachs, for example, forecasts 2018 S&P 500 EPS will jump by 14% to $150, of which 5% is the estimated impact of corporate tax cuts.[16] Beyond this, the long-term effects hinge on the degree to which tax incentives boost business capital spending and potential growth.

Views on this matter vary widely among economists. Among the most optimistic are Martin Feldstein, the chair of the Council of Economic Advisors in the Reagan years, and Kevin Hassett, the current chair. Feldstein, for example, has claimed that corporate tax reform could increase the US capital stock by $5 trillion and cause a $500 billion rise in annual income, while Hassett contends the

---

[15] See "G.O.P.'s Next Step: Cutting the Safety Net for Millions," *The New York Times*, December 3, 2017.

[16] See Goldman Sachs Portfolio Research Strategy, "2018 US Equity Outlook: Rational Exuberance," November 21, 2017.

expansion in business investment will boost average wage incomes by at least $4000 a year and possibly by as much as $9000 annually.[17] The leading critics are Larry Summers and Paul Krugman, who counter that these claims are gross exaggerations and who maintain the Republican tax plan is a serious policy error.[18]

One of the most informative discussions is "The Great Tax Debate" between Robert Barro, who supports the tax legislation, and Jason Furman and Larry Summers, who oppose it.[19] The analysis Barro provided *Project*

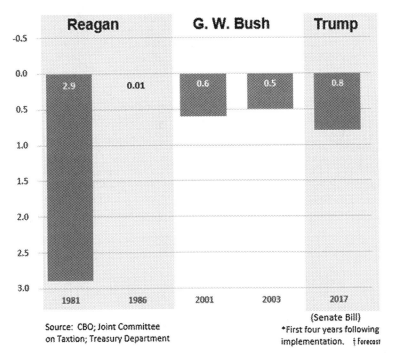

Trumped
United States, revenue effect of tax cuts
Four-year average*, % of GDP

Fig. 5.5 Revenue effects of tax cuts (% of GDP). (Source: The Economist)

[17] See Martin Feldstein, "Corporate Tax Reform Is the Key to Growth," *Wall Street Journal*, November 5, 2017, and Kevin Hassett, "Remarks Before the Tax Policy Center-Tax Foundation," October 5, 2017 and "White House economic analysis of GOP tax reform plan—CNBC.com," October 16, 2017.

[18] See Lawrence H. Summers, "The Trump administration's tax plan is an atrocity," *Washington Post*, October 8, 2017 and Paul Krugman, "The Biggest Tax Scam in History," *The New York Times*, November 27, 2017.

[19] See Project Syndicate, Robert J. Barro, "How US Corporate-Tax Reform Will Boost Growth," December 13, 2017, and Jason Furman and Lawrence H. Summers, "Robert Barro's Tax Reform Advocacy: A Response," December 15, 2017.

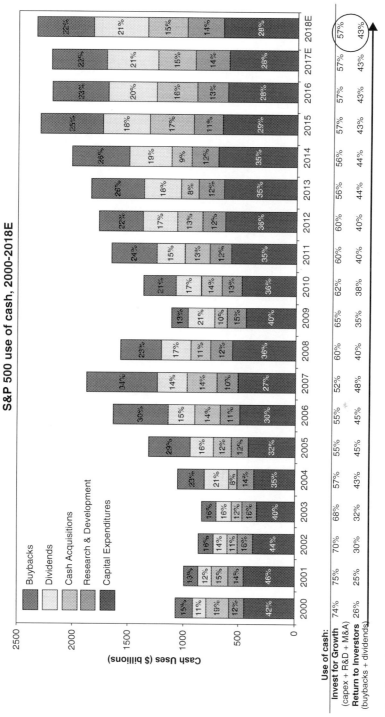

Fig. 5.6   S&P 500 use of cash, growth versus return to shareholders. (Source: Goldman Sachs)

Syndicate concluded that the tax legislation would boost the long-run level of economic output by 7%, which would imply an increase in the trend growth rate of 0.3% annually. Barro uses a standard model to first estimate the effect that a lower corporate tax rate and increased incentives will have on reducing the cost of capital, which in turn is projected to boost investment spending. He next calculates the effect an increase in the capital stock will have on raising the economy's potential output.

In their rebuttal, Furman and Summers accept the theoretical underpinnings of Barro's methodology, but they challenge the various parameters he assumes to base his calculations. They argue that Barro makes errors in modeling the actual tax provisions and that the parameters he selects distort his conclusions substantially upward: They contend that applying his methodology with their parameters would yield an increase in long-run growth of only 0.1% annually.

The consensus among economic forecasters is the legislation will have a moderate impact on boosting long-term growth in the vicinity of 0.1–0.2% annually, with most of the effects being front-loaded. One of the main challenges in trying to determine the economic impact is there have been only a few instances of comprehensive tax reform in the post-war era. The most significant were the Kennedy tax cuts in the mid-1960s and two rounds of tax changes during the Reagan years.

Of these, the most simulative was the 1981 tax cuts, which reduced tax revenues by nearly 3% of GDP on average over the first four years, and which caused the federal budget deficit to rise to more than 5% of GDP. By comparison, the current tax bill is estimated to reduce tax revenues by about 0.8% of GDP over the next four years (see Fig. 5.5). While the Reagan tax cuts were accompanied by an acceleration of economic growth, they occurred in an environment in which interest rates declined from record high levels as inflation and inflation expectations receded. Consequently, it is difficult to disentangle the effects of tax rate changes and interest rate changes on the economy.

One of the principal uncertainties in the current context is how effective lowering the cost of capital will be in spurring business investment. Over the past decade, there has been a marked increase in the share of free corporate cash flow that has been returned to investors in the form of buybacks and dividends, while the share going to capex, R&D and M&A has diminished (Fig. 5.6). Moreover, this occurred even as interest rates fell to record lows. Therefore, it remains to be seen whether tax rate cuts and incentives will be more effective in spurring capital spending and R&D. The bottom line is it is an empirical issue. There simply is not enough experience with tax cuts of the magnitude being undertaken to be confident of the outcome.

Impact on the Budget Deficit and Interest Rates

Another issue investors need to consider is the impact that the tax bill will have on the federal budget deficit and interest rates. Following the 2016 elections, it was unclear whether changes in the tax code would be designed to stimulate the economy as President Trump favored, or whether they would be part of broader reforms that would eliminate distortions and broaden the tax base, which House Republican leaders favored. Today, it is evident that a compromise was worked out, in which the net tax cut over the next ten years is targeted to be $1.4 trillion. This increase is considered to be moderate, as it is equivalent to 0.4% of GDP annually and well below estimates of proposals Trump put forth during the presidential campaign.

While the bond market did not respond to the pending legislation, the risk is that bond yields will rise in the future, as the federal budget deficit is expected to rise materially in the coming decade absent any policy changes. With the passage of the GOP tax plan, the deficit could expand by an additional $1 trillion according to the Joint Committee on Taxation beyond what is currently projected by CBO. Consequently, the timing of the tax cut has been called into question, as it occurs when the economy is close to full employment and also when the budget picture is expected to worsen in future years.

Concluding Assessment: A Complex Issue

This raises the fundamental issue: Is the tax legislation good or bad from an economic and market perspective? My own take is that it is very complex and should not be dismissed out of hand: There are both positive and negative features to the bill. Mickey Levy, Chief Economist of Berenberg Capital Markets, summarizes the trade-offs as follows[20]:

> A glass half-full assessment is that the legislation is a step forward from the current arcane tax system, particularly the sweeping changes in corporate taxes and the simplification of individual taxes; a glass-half empty assessment focuses on the legislation's weaknesses compared to the earlier "blueprints" for tax reform, its sun setting of key provisions, higher deficit projections, and the initial incidence of the legislation – the initial distribution by income bracket – without consideration of the economic responses to the policy changes.

Finally, while the long-term impact of the tax changes is debatable, most forecasters anticipate the legislation will boost real GDP growth in 2018—about 0.3 or so—mainly because the stimulus is front-end loaded. The Federal Reserve, for example, has revised its forecast of 2018 growth upward to 2.5% (Q4/Q4), but it sees growth subsequently slowing to 2.1% in 2019, indicating the effect is likely to be temporary. However, Mickey Levy offers the following perspective about why the effect of tax and regulatory reforms could be more enduring[21]:

[20] See Mickey Levy, "Tax Reform Legislation Observations," December 21, 2017.
[21] Ibid.

Our above-consensus forecast reflects the anticipated positive responses to the key provisions in the tax legislation plus the mounting benefits of the easing of burdensome regulations in an array of industries that are leading to more efficient production processes and heightened confidence. Many macroeconomic models (like the Fed's FRB-US) are underestimating how changes in the regulatory and tax policies are influencing economic outcomes because they estimate the impact of fiscal policy changes based primarily on the magnitude of the change in budget deficits while underestimating the positive efficiencies gained from reforms, and they do not fully capture how changes in the regulatory environment influence economic activity.

Equity investors appear to share this assessment: Throughout 2017, the US stock market was buoyed by improved performance of the economy and corporate profits, as well as by the prospect that changes in the tax code will provide an added boost. Going forward, the prospect for additional market gains hinges on whether it will provide the added lift that investors are expecting. An encouraging development in this regard is that business capital spending has accelerated this year, and business and consumer confidence readings are upbeat.

Meanwhile, investors should monitor the situation closely to ascertain how businesses are responding to the new tax incentives and regulatory changes. Amid all the political controversy over the tax bill, our view is that investors should have an open mind about its prospects for boosting capital spending, and then decide whether or not it is achieving its intended objective as new information unfolds. At this juncture, it is simply too early to tell.

CHAPTER 6

Macroeconomic Effects of Deregulation

In addition to tax cuts, the Trump administration is hoping to boost economic growth through reduced government regulations. This is an area in which many businesses have expressed frustrations over the past two decades. In a speech to the Economic Club of New York, Donald Trump mentioned that he frequently asks CEOs what they would pick if forced to choose between tax cuts and diminished regulations.[1] According to him, nine out of ten executives would opt to have fewer regulations. The reason: Companies can hire tax experts to navigate their way around the tax code, but it is far more difficult to circumvent regulations. The regulatory burden, moreover, is especially problematic for small businesses, and some observers contend it has hindered start-ups.

Businesses are not the only group who feel this way. Annual surveys conducted by Gallup show nearly half of Americans polled believe there is too much government regulation of business compared with 27% who think it is too little, although there is a wide divergence between Republicans and Democrats on this issue.

This chapter begins by considering the benefits and costs of regulation of businesses from a macroeconomic perspective. One of the main challenges is that most empirical research has focused on specific industries and a narrow set of regulations. There are few studies that assess the impact of regulations on the economy as a whole, and it is unclear how reliable the findings are. What is clear is the Trump administration has halted the onslaught of new regulations, and enforcement is much more business friendly than during the Obama administration.

The chapter next considers two key areas that impact the economy and which have been at the forefront of public policy—namely, the environment and financial services. One of the principal findings is that regulations in both areas have become overly complex and need to be streamlined. In the environmental sphere, market-based solutions have proved promising in dealing with

---

[1] September 20, 2016, Waldorf Astoria.

© The Author(s) 2018
N. P. Sargen, *Investing in the Trump Era*,
https://doi.org/10.1007/978-3-319-76045-2_6

acid rain, and prominent economists have proposed using them to tackle global warming. However, President Trump has not acquiesced because he is unconvinced there is a problem.

In the financial arena, the Trump administration is seeking to roll back restrictions imposed by the Dodd-Frank Act that are thought to hinder bank lending and to create "excess capital." The challenge policymakers confront is striking the proper balance between incenting banks to lend adequately while ensuring they do not risk the safety and soundness of the financial system.

Following Dodd-Frank's passage, investors perceived the legislation would make financial institutions become more like public utilities, and financial stocks materially underperformed the broad market for many years. More recently, financial stocks have performed in line with the broad market since President Trump's election amid expectations that regulations will be relaxed, and some equity analysts believe this pattern will continue as uncertainty about the new regulatory environment lessens.

Problems Regulations Pose for Small Businesses

While most businesses complain about government regulations, the group most adversely affected is small businesses. One reason is the rules cause them to incur fixed costs, and the scale of operations is much smaller than for larger firms. For example, a study by Nicole Crain and Mark Crain of Lafayette College estimates the cost per employee of complying with federal regulations at $10,585 for businesses with fewer than 20 employees compared with $7755 for businesses with more than 500 workers.[2] The researchers also contend that government regulations make small businesses less competitive against foreign firms. Other factors cited include increased uncertainty about how regulations could change and unintended consequences. For example, the ACA requires businesses to file 1099 forms for all payments exceeding $600 per year, which imposes heavy compliance costs that surprised many in Congress who supported the bill.

Nor does the United States fare well when compared with many industrialized nations. A study by the Organization for Economic Cooperation and Development (OECD) undertaken a decade ago found the United States had higher regulatory barriers to entrepreneurship, greater administrative burdens on small business owners and higher barriers to competition than a number of other industrialized countries.[3] An article in *The Economist* titled "Over-regulated America" made the following observation[4]:

> Americans love to laugh at ridiculous regulations...But red tape in America is no laughing matter. The problem is not the rules that are self-evidently absurd. It is the ones that sound reasonable on their own but impose a huge burden collectively.

[2] Nicole V. Crane and W. Mark Crane, "The Impact of Regulatory Costs on Small Firms," SBA, September 2010.

[3] Scott Shane, "Small Business's Problems with Government Regulation," Small Business Trends, January 31, 2011.

[4] *The Economist*, "Over-regulated America," February 18, 2012.

America is meant to be home to laissez-faire. Unlike Europeans, whose lives have long been circumscribed by meddling governments and diktats from Brussels, Americans are supposed to be free to choose, for better or worse. Yet for some time Americans have been straying from the ideal.

This begs the question about how costly regulations have been for the economy as a whole, and whether regulators always act in the best interest of consumers (see box on next page). The problem is no one really knows. The federal government is not required to track total regulatory costs, and most empirical studies by economists have focused on a narrow set of industries. Federal agencies are only required to conduct cost-benefit analyses on rules deemed "economically significant," which are defined as having an annual effect on the economy of at least $100 million. The Congressional Research Service, therefore, has warned that it is inherently difficult to estimate the total cost of regulations and that such estimates "should be used with a great deal of caution."[5]

While recognizing this caveat, we nonetheless find a 22-industry study by the Mercatus Center at George Mason University interesting.[6] It attempts to measure the cumulative costs of regulation over a long period and poses the counter-factual issue—what would have happened if federal regulations had been frozen at levels that prevailed in 1980. The authors contend the buildup in regulations since then has adversely impacted decision making relating to research and development, business expansion, capital spending and updating manufacturing processes. They estimate these factors have lowered overall economic growth by 0.8% per annum. If this estimate were reliable, it would suggest deregulation could boost the economy's growth rate significantly. However, there has been no validation of these results by outside sources, and many economists would view them as being very high. For example, researchers from George Washington University and the National Association of State Budget Officers conclude there is no basis to conclude their measure of federal regulation indicates it slows job creation or economic growth.[7]

What is clear is the Trump administration is serious about reducing regulatory burdens businesses face. It has done so thus far by instituting a regulatory freeze that has slowed the number of new regulations in effect considerably. For example, the Office of Information and Regulatory Affairs approved just 15 regulations between Inauguration Day and the end of May, by far the fewest in any comparable period during three prior administrations (Fig. 6.1) At the same time, the enforcement environment has been much more business friendly than during the Obama administration, and this is reflected in the favorable business confidence readings.[8]

---

[5] Congressional Research Service, March 27, 2017.

[6] Bentley Coffey, Patrick A. McLaughlin, and Pietro Peretto, "The Cumulative Cost of Regulations," Mercatus Center, George Mason University, April 2016.

[7] Regulatory Review, April 3, 2013.

[8] See Gerald F. Seib, "Trump's Deregulatory Juggernaut Is Rolling," Wall Street Journal, October 31, 2017.

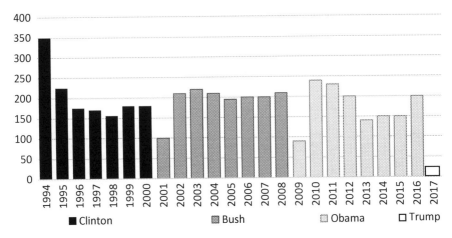

Fig. 6.1 Slowdown in federal regulations. (Source: Politico/Office of Information and Regulatory Affairs)

The Issue of Regulatory Capture

George Stigler, a Nobel laureate economist at the University of Chicago, pioneered analyzing the way regulatory policies worked in practice rather than theory. In his seminal article "The Theory of Economic Regulation" Stigler formulated the concept of "regulatory capture," which refers to the way regulators often behave.[9] Namely, as a result of the close affiliation they develop with businesses they oversee, Stigler observed that regulators often are co-opted—or "captured"—by those businesses and wind up protecting them.

An example is the Interstate Commerce Commission, which was created in 1887 to regulate railroads. At the time railroads were viewed as a natural monopoly, and the objective in creating the ICC was for it to set rates that would be more indicative of a competitive market. To do so, the ICC set rates based on calculations of marginal costs and a normal markup. The railroad industry was opposed to government intrusion until a US Attorney General advised them they could become more profitable by working with the Commission than by fighting it. This turned out to be true: During the 1930s, when railroads faced competition from truckers, they lobbied Congress to regulate the trucking industry. In this way, the original goal of regulating railroads became distorted, and the ICC effectively helped to protect railroads from other means of transportation.

(continued)

[9] George Stigler, "The Theory of Economic Regulation," *Bell Journal of Economics and Management Science*. 1971.

(continued)

Stigler's thinking on this topic was pervasive and caused economists to delve deeper into the impact that regulatory policies had on businesses. By and large, many economists who studied the impact on specific industries found that regulations often harmed the interests of consumers and in some instances increased the pricing power of businesses. Some of these findings provided impetus for economists to support deregulation of transportation, natural gas and banking, which gained momentum during the Carter administration and continued through the Reagan administration.

A recent example cited by John Taylor is the role regulatory capture played in the 2008 financial crisis.[10] Both Fannie Mae and Freddie Mac were empowered to prevent institutions from taking excessive risks in the mortgage area. However, beginning in the late 1990s both agencies guaranteed home mortgages that had a high probability of default. In their book *Reckless Endangerment*, Gretchen Morgenson and Joshua Rosen of the *New York Times* illustrate how government officials acted to benefit well-connected individuals who in turn helped the officials. Taylor observes: "This mutual-support system thwarted good economic policies and encouraged reckless ones. It thereby helped bring on the crisis, sending the economy into recession."[11]

Regulations Affecting the Environment and Financial Services

Much of the debate about regulatory policy today centers on federal regulations that are designed to protect consumers from environmental problems and from deleterious practices of financial institutions. In both areas the shortcomings of the regulatory processes stem from legislation that is overly complex and difficult to administer. Therefore, economists have been seeking ways to streamline the regulations and to create more market-based solutions to the problems.

Environmental Protection

One area that has seen a steady expansion of regulations is environmental policy. A wave of regulations occurred in the 1970s that resulted in the creation of the Environmental Protection Agency (EPA), OSHA and the Consumer Public Safety Act among others. The signature piece of legislation was the Clean Air Act, which authorized the development of comprehensive federal and state

[10] Taylor, op. cit., pp. 149–152.
[11] Ibid, p. 151.

regulations from both industrial sources and automobiles. It was followed by amendments to cover geographic areas that do not meet one or more of the federal quality standards in 1977 and legislation enacted in the early 1990s to deal with the problem of acid rain.

Considerable progress has been achieved in battling air and water pollution, which has improved human health and the environment. Nonetheless, a prevalent view today is environmental policy is extremely complex, has led to ungainly bureaucracies, has incurred high costs, is politically polarized and is also very litigious.[12] A report by the Brookings Institution on the 30th anniversary of the creation of the EPA, for example, acknowledged that US companies were complaining about the high cost of compliance, and it cited two studies that estimated the annual cost in the late 1990s to range between $144 billion and $185 billion.[13] Businesses have also complained the rules have outlived their usefulness, have resulted in job losses and make American companies less competitive internationally.

The problems, to a large extent, stem from the Clean Air Act being one of the first in a series of statutes that gave citizens the right to regulatory protection, to command agencies to do what is necessary to protect those rights and to direct courts to enforce the demands. During the 1970s, consumers and environmental groups also began to receive "intervention" or "public participation" funding to cover their costs for advocating before federal agencies in the public interest. As David Schoenbrod, Richard B. Stewart and Katrina M. Wyman of New York Law School observe:

> Environmental protection in the United States is increasingly stuck after several decades of significant but patchy and incomplete success. The shortcomings cannot be pinned entirely, or even primarily, on presidents getting too cozy with special interests. Multiple administrations under presidents of both parties have fallen well short of the goals of the environmental statutes. The statutes themselves are at the root of the problem.[14]

This view is shared by William E. Ruckelshaus, who served on two occasions as EPA administrator. Ruckelshaus wrote: "Any senior EPA official will tell you that the agency has the resources to do no more than ten percent of the things that Congress has charged it to do."[15] Nor is the problem a shortage of administrators: The EPA is the largest federal agency with approximately 20,000 employees, and Congress has empowered it to conscript a large number of state officials to enforce its requirements.

---

[12] See Donald F. Kettl, "Environmental Policy: The Next Generation," The Brookings Institution, October 1, 1998.

[13] Ibid.

[14] David Schoenbrod, Richard B. Stewart and Katrina M. Wyman, *Breaking the Logjam: Environmental Protection That Will Work*, Yale University Press, 2010.

[15] Ibid., p. 4.

According to David Schoenbrod, the environmental legislation allows elected officials to take credit for the benefits of legislation, while shifting blame to agencies for the burdens.[16] He contends the system became so politically profitable that politicians from both sides showed limitless enthusiasm for giving citizens' rights to protection. Schoenbrod points out that the Clean Air Act contained 940 detailed commands for the EPA to administer, and some require it to issue dozens of separate regulations that impact businesses.[17] In Schoenbrod's view, Americans can get regulatory statutes that give them less burden only if members of Congress bear personal responsibility for the consequences of the laws they enact.

Market-Based Solutions to Environmental Problems

What would better statutes entail? The consensus among experts is policymakers should seek market-oriented solutions to environmental problems. As Paul Portnoy and Robert Stavis observe in the second edition of their book, *Public Policies for Environmental Protection*, this is the direction environmental policy has been taking:

> These policy instruments, such as tradable permits, pollution charges, and deposit-refund systems, are often characterized as "harnessing market forces" because if they are well designed and implemented, they encourage firms (and/or individuals) to undertake pollution control efforts that are in their own interest and that collectively meet policy goals. In political terms, market-based instruments have by now moved center stage, and policy debates look very different from the time when these ideas were characterized as "licenses to pollute" or dismissed as impractical.[18]

The starting point is to recognize that pollution is an externality—that is, it is a side effect or consequence of an industrial or business activity that affects other parties without the cost being imputed. Figure 6.2 illustrates the application of this principle to set prices for products. The left side shows how prices would be set in a competitive market when social costs are excluded (S curve) and when they are included (S′) as businesses are taxed for polluting the environment. The right side illustrates how prices are set when the government sets restrictions on the total quantity of pollution that is allowed. The price is higher than a competitive market would charge, as it reflects the imputed social costs.

One application is the way Congress dealt with the problem of acid rain. Legislators felt pressure to reduce sulfur dioxide emissions from power plants, but they were reluctant to require plants to install pollution-removal equipment, because they would raise electricity rates to consumers and thereby anger voters. This situation gave rise to disputes between states where plants were

---

[16] David Schoenbrod, "Only Congress Can Undo Its Regulatory Mess," *Wall Street Journal*, June 19, 2017.

[17] Ibid.

[18] Paul R. Portnoy and Robert N. Stavis, *Public Policies for Environmental Protection*, 2nd edition, RFF Press, 2000.

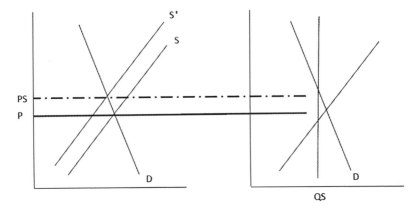

Fig. 6.2 Incorporating social costs into competitive markets

located (and who wanted to shift the cost to electricity consumers) and those in the states that complained about acid rain. The dispute ultimately led to regional conflicts, which in turn prevented the EPA and Congress from taking meaningful action for more than a decade. The impasse was broken in 1990 when Congress established a standard of conduct whereby each power plant would be granted an allowance for each ton of emissions. Congress also established an overall limit on allowances that were available, with the cap set to decline by 50% in 2010 from 1980 levels.

This approach became known as "cap and trade," because the government sets caps on the total amount of allowances and permits them to be traded between companies that emit sulfur dioxide. Economists favor this approach because it means that the reduction in emissions takes place at plants that can accomplish the goal most cheaply, which is consistent with efficient resource allocation. Also, because allowances command a positive price, firms are incented to reduce their emissions and profit by selling allowances.

According to Schoenbrod, Stewart and Wyman, cap and trade has been highly successful: It succeeded in achieving the goal of reducing overall emissions while saving consumers, plant holders and shareholders considerable costs relative to standard regulatory procedures. Furthermore, the entire cap and trade program is run by fewer than 50 people at the EPA.

By comparison, solutions to the problem of global warming have proven to be more difficult to implement in the United States. One reason is the problem was not known when the Clean Air Act was enacted in 1970. It has since been linked scientifically to greenhouse emissions such as carbon dioxide, methane and nitrous oxide. The main problem in dealing with global warming is that it arises from burning fossil fuels, which is basic to the economy and jobs. To burn less requires either constricting the economy, making it more energy efficient or providing alternative sources of energy.

For President Trump, the price of constraining the use of fossil fuels is deemed to be too great to justify the costs. However, the US government has not attempted to quantify the costs and benefits of restricting greenhouse emissions. (See the box on the next page for an attempt by the American Action Forum [AAF].) This could be achieved by creating a cap and trade system for them as with acid rain: It would provide businesses the latitude on where and how to do in the most economical ways, while creating incentives for the development of more efficient solutions.

An alternative solution is to tax carbon emissions. This idea has been forth by a group of former government officials—James A. Baker III, George P. Shultz and Henry M. Paulson—who contend it as a "conservative climate solution" that is based on free-market principles.[19] At an initial tax of $40 per ton of carbon dioxide produced, the tax would raise an estimated $200 billion to $300 billion a year, the proceeds of which could be returned to consumers as a "carbon dividend." The proposal would substitute the carbon tax for the Obama administration's Clean Power Plan, a complex set of regulations that President Trump has pledged to repeal and which is tied up in many court challenges. However, the Trump administration has failed to endorse the plan thus far.

Finally, an added challenge of dealing with global warming is that it requires a collective solution, because the positive effects of one country or a group of countries implementing measures to reduce emissions could be offset by countries that do not agree to such measures. This was the rationale for both the Kyoto Protocol and the Paris Climate Agreement from which the Trump administration opted to withdraw.

Cost-Benefit Analysis of Using Regulation to Achieve Climate Goals

The AAF, a center-right think tank, has conducted research that assesses the impact of government regulations on the economy. In a report issue in December 2016, AAF researchers arrived at the following conclusions relating to the costs and benefits of using regulation to achieve climate goals[20]:

- Using regulations to achieve 80% greenhouse gas (GHG) reductions would impose costs between $588 billion and $4.5 trillion, depending on policy goals and abatement costs, by 2050.
- The economic impacts of such high regulatory costs would (conservatively) reduce GDP by between 0.6% and 2.3% by 2050, with a cumulative economic loss ranging between $1.3 and $7.2 trillion.
- A regulatory approach to deep decarbonization is expensive, especially when compared to a revenue neutral carbon tax.

The report observes that the most economically efficient means of reducing GHG emissions is through a carbon tax. The reason: Market

(*continued*)

---

[19] John Schwartz, "A Conservative Climate Solution: Republican Group Calls for Carbon Tax," *The New York Times*, February 7, 2017.

[20] See Sam Batkins, Philip Rossetti, Dan Goldbeck, "The Costs and Benefits of Using Regulation to Achieve Climate Goals," American Action Forum, December 19, 2016.

(continued)

participants will naturally seek the lowest cost methods of abatement. However, it also acknowledges that a carbon tax is politically contentious, because of the deleterious effects on the economy if it is used as a tool to raise revenue. Therefore, the researchers recommend offsetting the tax increase:

> The EIA estimates the negative effect of a carbon tax ($20 per ton) increasing by 5% annually would be to reduce GDP by 0.2 to 0.4% from the baseline by 2040. However, when the same tax was assumed to be used to reduce business taxes, the economic effect was "near the reference level." This is consistent with the literature on carbon taxes, which indicates that if used to offset business and corporate taxes (the most distortionary taxes), the economic impact will be small, if anything.

Financial Sector Regulation

The considerations entailed in regulation of the financial sector are different than most other industries because of its importance to the overall economy and household savings. The history of the nineteenth century is replete with numerous US banking crises that resulted in people rushing to withdraw deposits before banks collapsed. Oversight of the banking industry became more prevalent when the Federal Reserve was established in 1913. However, the Fed encountered problems trying to stabilize the economy during the Great Depression, and a wave of regulations affecting financial services was enacted in the 1930s.

The most important was Glass-Steagall, which prohibited commercial banks from participating in the investment banking activities.[21] The act was passed in 1933 as an emergency measure to restore confidence in the banking system amid the failure of nearly 5000 banks. It was also believed that allowing banks to invest in securities they underwrote encouraged speculation and created a conflict of interest.

Glass-Steagall is generally credited as contributing to financial stability during the post-war period, when banking crises were few and far between.[22] Nonetheless, several factors coalesced to bring about its repeal. The first was the problem that high inflation in the 1970s and 1980s posed for commercial banks and thrift institutions that were subject to statutory limits on deposit

---

[21] Other regulatory agencies created at the time included the Federal Home Loan Bank Board to oversee savings and loan associations, the Federal Deposit Insurance Corporation to protect deposits and to regulate state chartered banks that were not members of the Federal Reserve, and the Security and Exchange Act that established the SEC.

[22] Two notable exceptions were the developing country debt crisis in the 1980s, which threatened the solvency of some of the largest commercial banks and required special measures to avert bankruptcies, and the savings and loan crisis during the 1980s and 1990s.

rates they were allowed to pay. These restrictions were eventually eliminated to lessen problems of disintermediation. Another factor was the impact globalization and financial liberalization abroad had on the US financial institutions. The US multinational banks and securities firms, for example, contended they were at a competitive disadvantage competing with universal banks that could conduct both commercial banking and investment banking activities. A third factor was the evolution of derivatives such as futures and options, which financial institutions claimed enabled them to better manage risks and therefore lessened the need for extensive regulations.

As capital markets evolved and became a more important source of finance in the 1980s, commercial banks redoubled their efforts to become involved in securities underwriting and M&A activity. They chipped away steadily, first being granted authority to underwrite municipal securities and eventually corporate debt and equity. Consequently, by the time Glass-Steagall was formally repealed in 1999, many regarded it as an afterthought. However, as discussed below, some observers contended the repeal was responsible for the GFC that ensued.

Underlying Causes of the GFC

The case for increased regulation of the financial system following the GFC is that it was a consequence of market failure. This view was the majority opinion of the Financial Crisis Inquiry Commission (FCIC) that was formed to investigate the causes of the crisis and to make recommendations to enhance the safety and soundness of the financial system. The origins of the crisis were attributed to a bubble in housing and a breakdown in the process of securitizing mortgages: "It was the collapse of the housing bubble—fueled by low interest rates, easy and available credit, scant regulation, and toxic mortgages—that was the spark."[23] The severity of the crisis, in turn, was attributed to failures of corporate governance and risk management at many systemically important financial institutions.

The FCIC report also concluded that widespread failures in financial regulation and supervision proved devastating to the stability of financial markets:

> The sentries were not at their posts, in no small part due to the widely accepted faith in the self-correcting nature of the markets and the ability of financial institutions to effectively police themselves...More than 30 years of deregulation and reliance on self-regulation by financial institutions championed by former Federal Reserve Chairman Alan Greenspan and others, supported by administrations and Congresses, and actively pushed by powerful industry at every turn, had stripped away key safeguards, which could have helped avoid catastrophe.[24]

---

[23] The Financial Crisis Inquiry Report submitted by The Financial Crisis Inquiry Commission, January 2011, Official Government edition.

[24] Ibid, p. xviii.

A dissenting opinion countered that the United States was not the only country to experience a credit bubble. It criticized the majority view for "focusing too narrowly on US regulatory policy and supervision, ignoring international parallels, emphasizing only arguments for greater regulation, failing to prioritize the causes, and failing to distinguish sufficiently between causes and effects."[25]

For some observers, the FCIC's findings are moot, because Congress already had passed the Dodd-Frank Act six months before the report was released. At first blush, many of the goals of Dodd-Frank seem laudatory: Providing better consumer protection from abusive financial practices, ending bank bailouts, creating an early warning system, and improving transparency and accounting for exotic instruments. However, many observers are skeptical that Dodd-Frank can produce the desired results. Among the principal criticisms are the following:

- The bill is too complex. It contains 849 pages of legislation and several thousand pages in subsequent rule-making documentation. One provision alone—namely, the so-called Volcker rule that would restrict proprietary trading has yet to be implemented years later.
- It has proved to be very costly with uncertain benefits. A study by the AAF concluded that at the end of its sixth anniversary Dodd-Frank had imposed more than $36 billion in cost on the financial services industry and 73 million hours of paperwork.[26] Moreover, as time passes the law will become more expensive and burdensome.
- It imposes significant new restrictions on activities of many banks, insurance companies and other financial institutions that had little to do with the crisis. As a result, it could result in regulatory overkill.
- It is unlikely to protect against the next financial crisis. One of the key objectives of Dodd-Frank, for example, is to mitigate the risk of "Too Big to Fail." However, Charles Calomiris of the Columbia Business School contends the provision to provide for orderly liquidation of insolvent institutions is unworkable and that the path of least resistance remains bailouts.[27] Furthermore, the banking industry has become even more concentrated since the GFC, with the top five US banks today accounting for nearly one half of all deposits, as compared with 30% before the crisis.

What can be done to address these issues? Views on this matter are diverse depending on one's perspective about the factors contributing to the financial crisis and possible remedies. The approach the US Treasury has advocated

---

[25] Ibid., p. 421.

[26] Sam Batkins, Dan Goldbeck, "Six Years After Dodd-Frank: Higher Costs, Uncertain Benefits," American Action Forum, July 20, 2016.

[27] Charles W. Calomiris, "Four Principles for Replacing Dodd-Frank," *The Wall Street Journal*, June 16, 2017.

would redress what it sees as a problem Dodd-Frank has created: Namely, it contends Dodd-Frank has discouraged banks from extending credit to small businesses and that it has created "an excess of capital."

In reviewing these issues, however, some observers have challenged Treasury's claim that regulations have resulted in slower growth of credit.[28] In the aftermath of the GFC, for example, there was a significant contraction of credit during 2009–2010, which is attributed to a decline in loan demand on the part of businesses and a self-imposed tightening in lending standards by financial institutions. But it is more difficult to isolate an effect that Dodd-Frank has had on overall lending since it was enacted. Data compiled by the Bank for International Settlements show that after plateauing relative to GDP from 2011 to 2014, the pace of US bank lending to nonfinancial corporate businesses accelerated beginning in 2015 and has been on a rising trend since then.

Also, while it is often asserted that banks have been constrained from making loans to small businesses due to restrictions, the Fed's quarterly survey of senior loan officers does not point to an unusual pattern of credit tightening since Dodd-Frank was enacted.

The biggest changes under consideration by the Treasury would alleviate capital and liquidity requirements for the largest banks. According to the US Treasury there is now an "excess of capital" that constrains the supply of bank credit, and it calls for a "recalibration" in cases where regulators have set requirements on the largest US banks that are in excess of international standards. Yet the institutions that became troubled during the GFC were ones that sought to boost overall profitability via excessive financial leverage and which funded the purchase of illiquid instruments with short-term borrowings. The trigger for disaster was the value of their assets plummeted when the housing bubble burst, and the impact was magnified by the need to de-lever their balance sheets quickly at fire sale prices.

Consequently, some experts are concerned that the Treasury's proposals could move too far in the direction of loosening capital and liquidity standards. For example, Kim Schoenholtz of NYU observes:

> Only 8 years after the end of the worst financial crisis since the Great Depression, the U.S. Treasury has shifted from becoming a leading proponent for enhancing the resilience of the global financial system to an advocate for the private interests of a few financial behemoths in the name of boosting growth…We can only hope that in the future, we won't look back at Treasury's shift as the start of a trend that once again makes our financial system highly vulnerable to severe disruption.

[28] See Kim Schoenholtz, Money, Banking and Financial Markets, "The Treasury's Missed Opportunity," June 19, 2017.

The bottom line is that while there is a strong case for lessening the regulatory burden of Dodd-Frank, there is also a risk the pendulum could swing back too far in the direction of lessening capital and liquidity requirements, which would leave the financial system exposed to unforeseen risks.

IMPLICATIONS FOR BANK STOCKS

From a market perspective, the GFC and its aftermath proved to be a toxic environment for bank stocks and other financials. As a group, the financial sector materially underperformed the broad market from the onset of the crisis in 2008 until the November 2016 election (see Fig. 6.3). This reflected a combination of forces at play. First, the profitability of financial institutions was crushed by losses on holdings of securities and loans throughout the crisis period. Second, record low interest rates, a relatively flat yield curve and narrow credit spreads hampered financial institutions' ability to boost earnings significantly. Third, the increased regulatory burdens imposed by Dodd-Frank restricted the flexibility of financial institutions to adapt to an environment of

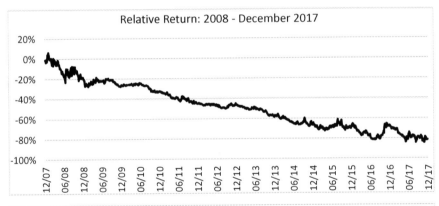

Fig. 6.3   Performance of financial stocks relative to the S&P 500 index

slower credit expansion. In fact, many investors concluded that the aim of the regulations was effectively to make financial institutions behave more like regulated utilities.

In the aftermath of the 2016 election, financial stocks surged initially through the end of 2016 and then performed in line with the broad market during 2017 for the first time in nearly a decade. This partly was due to the perception that the Trump administration would seek to roll back Dodd-Frank, while also lessening regulatory oversight of financial institutions. In addition, financial stocks benefitted from expectations that stronger growth would enable the Federal Reserve to begin normalizing interest rates. Although financials underperformed in the second quarter of 2017, as investors perceived the Fed would slow the pace of policy tightening, the sector still finished the year 19% higher, which was in line with the broad index. Looking ahead, it is generally agreed the performance of financial stocks is closely tied to the performance of the economy and to the path of interest rates.

PART III

Monetary, Exchange Rate and Trade Policies

CHAPTER 7

Changes in US Monetary Policy: Past and Prospective

One issue that was not debated during the 2016 election was the conduct of US monetary policy. This is not unusual: It stems from the Federal Reserve being created as an independent government agency in which monetary policy decisions are not subject to approval by the President or anyone in the executive or administrative branches of government.[1] The Fed is ultimately accountable to the public and Congress, which established the statutory objectives of maximum sustainable employment and stable prices—the so-called dual mandate—in the Federal Reserve Act.

While the Federal Reserve is an independent entity, the President of the United States plays an important role in nominating appointments for the Board of Governors to serve 14-year terms, as well as the chair, who serves a four-year term. What is unusual in the current context is the influence President Trump has in filling five positions on the Board (out of seven members) including selecting the next Fed chair and vice chair. Also, with Bill Dudley's retirement from the New York Federal Reserve, there will be a new troika running the organization.

This chapter begins by reviewing the Fed's greatest achievement over the past four decades—namely, reining in inflation and inflation expectations in the early 1980s under Paul Volcker's leadership and continuing with Alan Greenspan. This set the stage for a steady decline in interest rates that fueled the economy and financial markets until 1999.

As inflation declined, however, credit expansion proliferated and a series of asset bubbles ensued, which culminated in the 2008 Global Financial Crisis and Great Recession.

---

[1] The Fed was structured to ensure monetary policy decisions are not subject to political pressures that could lead to undesirable outcomes; hence, members of the Board of Governors are appointed for staggered 14-year terms, and the Board chair is appointed by the President for a four-year term.

© The Author(s) 2018
N. P. Sargen, *Investing in the Trump Era*,
https://doi.org/10.1007/978-3-319-76045-2_7

Since then, the Fed under Ben Bernanke and Janet Yellen has engaged in unorthodox monetary policies called quantitative easing (QE) that increased the Fed's balance sheet fourfold. Although Fed officials view these policies as being successful in countering deflation and lowering unemployment, they are controversial because they distort market prices and raise uncertainty about how they will be unwound. This chapter examines the debate surrounding QE and efforts to normalize interest rates, including the risk that something could go awry.

Finally, the chapter concludes by considering how the conduct of monetary policy could be altered by the appointment of Jerome Powell as chair along with a new leadership team. The consensus view among market participants is that Powell was a "safe" choice, because he favors staying with the current course of monetary, while he is less committed to extensive regulation of the financial sector than Janet Yellen. One of the big unknowns is what the Fed's stance will be on asset bubbles and, in particular, whether it continues the practice of injecting liquidity whenever the stock market sells off. It also remains to be seen how the Fed will respond once the economic expansion falters.

FED POLICY IN THE ERA OF HIGH INFLATION

It is widely accepted today that monetary policy is among the most important factors for market participants to consider in positioning investment portfolios. The reason: The Fed plays a critical role in setting interest rates, which are key determinants of bond yields, stock prices and exchange rates. No other variable has as great of an influence on each of these markets. Consequently, market participants devote considerable time and energy to examine factors that influence the Fed's policy decisions.

This was not always the case. When Keynesian economics reigned in the 1960s, for example, many economists viewed fiscal policy as pre-eminent, especially in the wake of the Kennedy tax cuts that were viewed to have been successful in boosting the economy. By comparison, monetary policy was generally considered to be less powerful. One reason is Fed policy was ineffective in combatting the Great Depression, which gave rise to the view that monetary policy was akin to "pushing on a string."[2] Another reason is inflation was low and steady during the post-war era through the mid-1960s—in the vicinity of 2% or less—and bond yields did not fluctuate much. Consequently, investors were content to hold bonds to maturity and clip the coupons.

During the 1960s, Milton Friedman stood out as the leading proponent of monetarism. His message was twofold. First, money matters. However, he believed monetary policy worked with long and variable lags that typically last at least two years. Second, it is better to rely on rules in setting policy than to

---

[2] The Keynesian interpretation is that monetary policy was ineffective when interest rates were close to zero—the so-called liquidity trap. The monetarist response, however, is that Fed policy was too restrictive and by allowing banks to fail, the Fed permitted the money supply to collapse.

rely on discretion. Specifically, Friedman advocated that policymakers should target money supply growth to be in line with GDP growth.

Monetarism came into vogue in the 1970s when the world of low inflation and low interest rates ended abruptly. After the Bretton Woods system collapsed in the early 1970s, central banks no longer were constrained to maintain a fixed parity with respect to gold in setting exchange rates.[3] Soon after, prices for oil and other commodities surged, and wages and prices accelerated. Central banks responded by increasing short-term interest rates, but not enough to curb inflation expectations or to contain wage increases. As a result, interest rates were negative after adjusting for inflation expectations, and the period from the early 1970s to the early 1980s came to be known as The Great Inflation.

When Paul Volcker assumed the helm as Fed chair in late 1979, he realized gradualism was not working, and he embarked on an experiment in which the federal funds rate was allowed to rise to levels that would clear the market for bank reserves. The effects were profound, as interest rates spiked to record levels—20% for short-term rates and as high as 14% for bond yields—while fluctuating considerably in the interim.

The US economy ultimately succumbed in 1982, when a severe recession ensued and many less developed countries (LDCs) were unable to service their external debt. The experience was very painful, especially as the US unemployment rate reached 10.8%, the highest since the Great Depression. However, the Fed's resolve succeeded in breaking the back of inflation expectations, and bond yields plummeted, setting the stage for a powerful stock market rally that lasted until late 1987.

The Great Moderation

By comparison, Alan Greenspan, who served as Fed chairman from August 1987 through January 2006, presided during a period of unusual economic calm that his successor, Ben Bernanke, called "The Great Moderation."[4] During this period, the quarterly volatility of real GDP (measured by one standard deviation) declined by half, while the volatility of inflation decreased by two-thirds. In the process, the Fed and other central banks succeed in achieving their inflation targets of 2% while business cycle forces were also tamed (Fig. 7.1).

Critics of central bank policies, however, were concerned that the authorities largely ignored the issue of asset bubbles and financial market instability. This problem first appeared in Japan in the early 1990s, before spreading to Southeast Asia in 1997–1998 and then to the United States during the tech

---

[3] For a further discussion, see Nicholas Sargen, *Global Shocks*, Chap. 2.

[4] Benjamin Bernanke, "The Great Moderation," Board of Governors of the Federal Reserve System, February 20, 2004.

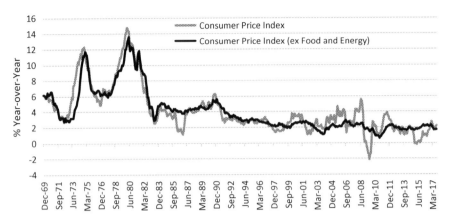

Fig. 7.1 The Fed succeeds in reining in inflation, 1970 to 2017. (Source: Federal Reserve)

bubble that burst in 2000.[5] In each case, the origins can be traced to easy credit market conditions and a rapid buildup in debt. In the United States, for example, nonfinancial debt of the private sector surged for three decades.

Following the bursting of the tech bubble, the Fed lowered the Federal funds rate to a then record low of 1% and kept rates unusually low even when the economy emerged from a mild recession. In an address before the Federal Reserve Symposium in Jackson Hole in August 2003, William White of the Bank for International Settlements urged central banks to take into account the effects their low interest rate policies could have on fostering asset bubbles. White concluded it was appropriate for policymakers to lean against the wind when asset prices were rising rapidly.[6]

The Federal Reserve chose to ignore these warnings, and it pursued a strategy of raising interest rates very gradually—by 25 basis points a quarter for 17 consecutive quarters. By 2005, it was evident the economy had regained momentum and the stock market had recovered most of the value lost during the 2000–2002 time frame. In the process the seeds were sown for a sizable expansion of credit that fueled an unprecedented rise in housing prices.

For their part, Fed officials contended their responsibility was to pursue the objectives of the dual mandate. They questioned their own ability and that of others to detect asset bubbles in advance, and Alan Greenspan maintained it was better for the Fed to wait for a bubble to burst and then to inject liquidity into the financial system to limit the fallout. He did so on several occasions, first

---

[5] Among the foremost critics were William White and Claudio Borio of the Bank for International Settlements, who repeatedly warned that excessive credit creation had increased the risk of financial instability.

[6] William White, Bank for International settlements, "Wither Monetary and Financial Stability? The Implications of Evolving Policy Regimes," presented at Jackson Hole, Wyoming Symposium, August 28–30, 2003.

after the October 1987 stock market crash, next during the market flare-up in September 1998 over the failure of Long Term Capital Management and once again in the early 2000s after the bursting of the tech bubble. As a result, some observers claimed the Fed's policies encouraged investors to take added risks, because they could count on the so-called Greenspan put to bail them out.

COMBATTING DEFLATION WITH QUANTITATIVE EASING (QE)

During the 2008 financial crisis, US monetary policy underwent a transformation comparable to the one Paul Volcker undertook in the early 1980s. This time, the Federal Reserve's objective was to stabilize the financial system, and the Fed injected an unprecedented volume of reserves into the system to counter de-leveraging by financial institutions. The intent was to bolster the economy and to lessen the risk of deflation.

As evidence mounted in 2007 that US housing prices were declining and institutions that issued subprime mortgages were in trouble, the Federal Reserve was slow to react and it did not begin to ease monetary policy until autumn. Thereafter, the pace of easing picked up in early 2008 when Bear Stearns failed, but policymakers at the Fed and other regulatory bodies failed to grasp the systemic nature of the problem.

Only when panic set in after Lehman Brothers was allowed to fail and money market funds encountered problems with redemptions did policymakers act decisively. Fed chair Ben Bernanke had studied mistakes that were made during the Great Depression and those by the BOJ following the bursting of the Japanese bubble, and he knew what to do. He realized that once a panic sets in and institutions and individuals hoard cash, the central bank must stand ready to supply liquidity at low interest rates. The Fed did so by purchasing massive amounts of government securities and residential mortgage-backed securities (RMBS). By expanding its balance sheet, the Fed was able to create substantial excess reserves in the banking system and also to provide liquidity for RMBS.

Some observers at the time were concerned that the buildup in bank reserves would eventually lead to inflation. However, this issue proved to be false, as banks did not convert the reserves into loans. Consequently, money supply growth did not reaccelerate (see Fig. 7.2). Rather, the initial round of QE worked as it was supposed to—namely, the credit crunch that occurred after the Lehman Brothers failure abated as counter-party risks lessened. This became apparent as a key measure of credit risk within the banking sector—the London Interbank Offered Rate-Overnight Indexed Swap rate (LIBOR-OIS) spread—fell back to levels before the financial crisis.[7]

The Fed's response to the GFC is widely credited by economists as having stabilized the financial system, and thereby averted an even worse outcome.

---

[7] Two other policy developments also helped restore confidence in the financial system. One was the conversion of the Troubled Asset Relief Program (TARP) into a vehicle to inject capital into financial institutions. The other was stress tests of financial institutions ability to absorb shocks that were conducted by the Federal Reserve.

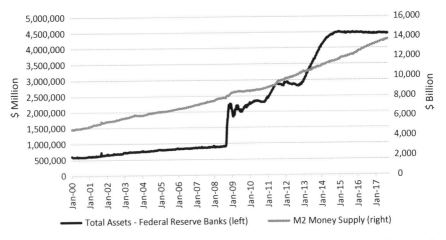

Fig. 7.2   Federal Reserve assets and the US money supply. (Source: Federal Reserve)

However, subsequent rounds of QE have been viewed more skeptically by many economists. The reason is they occurred when the economy had stabilized and interest rates already were at record lows.

The Fed's intent was encourage investors to hold more risk assets such as corporate stocks and bonds, which would bolster economic activity by creating a positive effect on household net worth. From the Fed's perspective, it was worth pursuing this policy in order to reduce the unemployment rate, which fell from a peak of 10% to nearly 4% at the end of 2017. One of the criticisms, however, is that its actions also distorted capital market prices and may have laid the foundations for yet another asset bubble. Previously, the Fed primarily influenced short-term interest rates, rather than the entire maturity structure, so it would not distort capital market allocations.

NORMALIZING MONETARY POLICY

The ultimate test of the QE experiment is the Fed's ability to develop a successful exit strategy. The Fed's staff has been working on a game-plan since the early part of this decade. One of the first steps the Fed took in this regard was its decision to pay interest on bank reserves. By doing so, the Fed created an additional means to control bank reserves and thereby lessen the risk that the money supply would expand unduly once bank-lending volumes picked up.

Officials are also cognizant of the mistake their predecessors made during the Great Depression, when the Fed worried that excess reserves could make it difficult to tighten policy if inflation developed. The Fed subsequently doubled reserve requirements in mid-1936, and banks reacted by reducing the volume of loans outstanding. According to Milton Friedman and Anna Schwartz, the resultant contraction in money supply was a central cause of the 1937–1938 recession that prolonged the Great Depression.[8]

One of the key differences today is that monetary policy works through the capital markets, as well as through the banks. Fed policy, for example, is now designed to affect capital market prices including short-term and long-term government bond yields, credit spreads versus treasuries, the level of the stock market and the trade-weighted value of the dollar. (See the discussion of the financial conditions index [FCI] as a gauge of the overall tightness of monetary policy on page 103). Therefore, the Fed ultimately must influence investors' expectations about the future by communicating its intensions clearly. Policymakers learned this lesson all too well during the so-called taper tantrum in mid-2013, when Ben Bernanke mentioned in Congressional testimony that the Fed was considering winding down its purchases of securities by the following year. Much to the Fed's surprise, bond yields surged by a full percentage point during the remainder of 2013. Thereafter, Fed officials went out of their way to reassure investors that a slowdown in asset purchases was not the same as a tightening in monetary policy in which securities are sold and reserves are drained from the system.

The Fed began to phase down its purchases of securities one year later, but it waited until the end of 2015 to raise the funds rate by one quarter of a percentage point, the first tightening of policy in nearly a decade. Thereafter, it waited a full year to move again before raising the funds rate three times in 2017. Markets reacted calmly throughout the process, mainly because the moves were telegraphed well in advance.

In addition to raising short-term rates, the Fed also began the process of shrinking its balance sheet incrementally in September 2017 while pausing in raising rates. In the process it made clear it would not be selling securities outright, but would allow a portion to roll off its books as bonds mature. At the June Federal Open Market Committee (FOMC) meeting, the Fed indicated the balance sheet would eventually decline by $50 billion on a monthly basis ($600 billion annually) until it chooses to halt or reverse the process. At this pace, the monetary base would fall back to its pre-crisis trend growth path by 2021. However, market participants do not expect it will get there: The consensus view is the Fed will aim for a balance sheet of $2.5 trillion to $3.0 trillion. The reasoning is that several factors have boosted the demand for reserves in the meantime including (i) payment of interest on bank reserves, (ii) diminished inflation expectations and (iii) increased demand for risk-free assets since the GFC.

It remains to be seen how well the transition to policy normalization will go. Although the initial process has been relatively smooth, the Fed nonetheless

---

[8] Milton Friedman and Anna Schwartz, *A Monetary History of the United States*, Princeton University Press, 1963.

faces formidable challenges ahead. One is to ascertain the natural rate of unemployment, commonly referred to as non-accelerating inflation rate of unemployment (NAIRU), below which inflation rises. This is important because the Fed utilizes econometric models, which assume the Phillips curve relationship between wage increases and unemployment holds. The problem is the relationship is far from stable: Normally, wage pressures would be evident with the unemployment rate well below 5%, but this has not happened. One reason may be that there is a large pool of workers who are currently working part time that may be seeking full-time jobs.

The issue investors ultimately care about is what level the federal funds rate will reach before the Fed pauses in tightening policy. Under normal circumstances, it would aim for a funds rate that is in line with the growth of nominal GDP. Thus, if the economy continues to expand close to the 2% trend rate of the past decade and inflation eventually reaches the Fed's 2% target, a funds rate in the vicinity of 4% would be reasonable. However, most observers believe the Fed will pause well before then—most likely once the funds rate reaches 2%. At the start of 2018, for example, the bond market was pricing in fewer rate hikes than Fed officials were expecting in the FOMC minutes (see Fig. 7.3). The reason: There is still considerable uncertainty whether the 2% inflation target will be reached, and investors presume the Fed does not want to risk undermining the expansion. Among the indicators market participants will be gauging in assessing the transition are the shape of the yield curve, credit spreads and the path of the money supply.

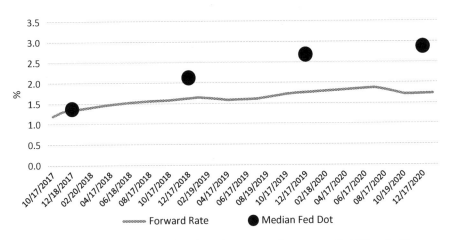

Fig. 7.3 Prospective rate hikes: bond market expectations versus Fed "Dots". (Source: Federal Reserve)

How Restrictive Is US Monetary Policy?

With the Federal Reserve now in process of gradual raising short-term interest rates and scaling back the size of its balance sheet, most observers would accept that the US monetary policy is being tightened gradually. However, by one commonly used yardstick—the FCI—a case can be made that monetary policy is still very accommodative (Fig. 7.4). As constructed by Goldman Sachs, the FCI contains measures of short-term and long-dated government bond yields, corporate credit spreads, the level of the stock market and the trade-weighted value of the dollar. These variables are affected by the conduct of monetary policy, and they, in turn, impact the real economy. Near the end of 2017, the FCI approached its lowest level since its inception, as government bond yields were relatively low, credit spreads were very narrow, the stock market stood at a record high, while the US dollar had softened on a trade-weighted basis since the beginning of the year. Collectively, these variables suggested credit market conditions were easy, and they were supportive of the economy.

Fig. 7.4 Financial conditions suggest monetary policy is accommodative. (Source: Goldman Sachs)

While these conditions bode well for the economy's performance in the near term, one caveat is that the FCI may be subject to a quick reversal should investors' expectations shift for any reason. During the events preceding the 2008 financial crisis, for example, asset prices for equities and credit plummeted, and the FCI surged (indicating a tightening in financial conditions). Consequently, the measure is best understood as reflecting conditions at a point in time that may or may not be indicative of where markets and the economy are headed.

How Might Monetary Policy Be Changed?

As noted at the outset, one issue that market participants weighed in the autumn of 2017 was how, if at all, the conduct of monetary policy might be altered by the appointment of a new Fed chair. The consensus view at the time was President Trump's selection of Jerome Powell was a "safe choice," because Powell has served on the Fed's Board since 2012, and he is in the camp that favors a gradual tightening of monetary policy. By comparison, two other candidates—John Taylor and Kevin Warsh—were regarded as more likely to alter the course of monetary policy. Also, while Powell's stance on monetary policy is close to that of Janet Yellen, President Trump reportedly picked him because he is a Republican and is less inclined to favor government regulation of the financial sector.

The most likely outcome, therefore, is the Fed is not about to change course significantly under Powell's term. Nonetheless, the changing composition of the Board—with four new Governors to be installed by 2018—and a new head of the New York Fed afford an opportunity to consider several important policy issues including the following: (i) Should the inflation target be changed? (ii) Should financial stability become an explicit goal of monetary policy? (iii) To what extent should the Board rely on explicit rules in setting monetary policy?

Altering the Inflation Target

The Federal Reserve and many other central banks now have set targets of 2% inflation in place to ensure there is no return to the period of high inflation in the 1970s and 1980s. As central banks succeeded in achieving their goal, they were pleased with the results in which declining inflation was accompanied by falling bond yields, rising stock prices and longer economic expansions. However, problems ensued following the GFC, as inflation rates fell below the 2% targeted levels and bond yields fell to record lows. Economic recoveries proved to be subpar, partly because there were limits to which interest rates could fall below zero. This situation gave rise to the secular stagnation thesis discussed in Chap. 2, in which real interest rates are too high to boost investment demand.

Proponents of the secular stagnation view such as Larry Summers and Paul Krugman have argued that in such circumstances central banks should raise their inflation targets to as much as 4%, such that real interest rates would be negative. Thus far, however, no central bank has taken up the call. First, most central bankers fear that if inflation expectations rose as a result of the change in the target level, it would be difficult to contain them, and they are in no mood to do so after the hard-fought battle with inflation in the 1970s and 1980s. Second, now is not a good time to experiment, considering that the US economy is on solid footing and unemployment is close to an all-time low. Therefore, it is very unlikely the new members of the Fed would favor such action, although they might consider whether it is desirable to set an acceptable band around a 2% target.

Taking Financial Stability into Account

A second issue to be considered is whether the Fed should take financial stability into account in setting monetary policy. As noted previously, both Alan Greenspan and Ben Bernanke rejected this idea, because they believed it was difficult, if not impossible, to anticipate when a bubble would burst. They contended it was preferable to flood the financial system with liquidity afterwards. The logic for this view is supported by the Japanese experience in the 1990s: The BOJ actively first sought to burst the bubble in real estate and the stock market by tightening monetary policy aggressively, but it failed to ease policy in the aftermath, which ultimately set the stage for deflation.

The counterargument is that while it may be risky for a central bank to take action to burst a bubble, it nonetheless should be cognizant of conditions that typically give rise to asset bubbles and then "lean against the wind" or take other steps to ameliorate the situation. Research undertaken by the Bank for International settlements (BIS), for example, has identified the linkage between rapid credit expansion and asset bubbles, as well as the critical role speculation in the property sector plays in financial crises due to the banking system being overly exposed to real estate and highly levered. Thus, William White and Claudio Borio have argued that central banks need to take credit expansion (and debt creation) into account in setting monetary policy, rather than being pre-occupied with inflation in the market for goods and services.

Rules Versus Discretion

One of the oldest debates in economics is about whether central banks should set policy based on rules or be free to use their discretion. It is relevant today amid criticisms of market-oriented economists that Fed policy has become very erratic and unpredictable in the past two decades.

A leading advocate for a rules-based approach is John Taylor of Stanford University, who was in the running for the Fed chair. In the early 1990s, Taylor formulated a rule that links the federal funds rate to two variables—(i) the difference between the actual inflation rate and the targeted rate, and (ii) the difference between the level of real GDP and potential GDP. Taylor demonstrated that this formula was a good predictor of the federal funds rate until the early 2000s, when the Fed kept rates unusually low to counter potential deflation risks, and during the aftermath of the GFC.

In his book, *First Principles*, Taylor does not assert that the Fed should adopt his own rule to set policy. Rather, he argues that the Fed should be required to submit a report to Congress on a rule or rules it follows in setting interest rates. From 1978 on, the Fed did so by specifying its targets for money supply growth. However, when the reporting requirements for money growth were dropped in 2000, nothing comparable was put in its place about interest rate reporting.

According to Taylor, a rule-like approach for setting interest rates is important to limit the Fed's discretion and to establish guidelines for accountability:

> The proposal does not require that the Fed choose any particular rule for the interest rate, only that it establish some rule and report what the rule is.

> But if the Federal Reserve deviates from its chosen strategy, the chairman of the Federal Reserve must provide a written explanation and answer questions at a public congressional hearing.[9]

The intent of Taylor's proposal is to put some boundaries on the Fed's discretion and a degree of control by Congress without day-to-day oversight of monetary policy operations. For their part, Fed officials contend that in basing interest rate decisions, they utilize econometric models for forecasting. However, these models have been notoriously poor at capturing turning points in the economy, and since the expansion began in mid-2009, the Fed's projections of economic growth and interest rates have been too high consistently. Indeed, the bond market has done a better job of predicting the funds rate than Fed officials have! In the end, the main argument for rejecting rules is that adherence to them could result in a worse outcome when there are structural changes in the economy and financial system.

Conclusion

The conduct of the US monetary policy has been among the most important factors influencing the US economy and financial markets for the past four decades. The Fed's greatest accomplishment has been to win the hard-fought battle to contain inflation, while its greatest challenge has been to contend with a series of asset bubbles that culminated in the GFC, which jeopardized the stability of the financial system. Following that experience, the Fed altered monetary policy in ways that had never been foreseen before, as it sought to influence capital market prices to encourage greater risk taken by investors. While the Fed was able to stabilize the financial system and to contribute to a significant decline in unemployment, the open issue is how successful it will be in normalizing interest rates and shrinking its balance sheet. While a new leadership team will likely continue the gradualist approach to policy normalization, it remains to be seen how it will respond to financial market sell-offs and to the risk of recession or higher inflation.

[9] Ibid, p. 132.

CHAPTER 8

Trade Imbalances and Jobs: A Macro Perspective

One of the hallmarks of Donald Trump's theme of America First is the need to restore lost jobs in manufacturing owing to unfair foreign competition. During the presidential campaign Trump criticized NAFTA and the Trans Pacific Partnership (TPP), and he threatened to impose heavy duties on imports from China, Mexico and other countries that are deemed to harm American workers. This stance raised alarm bells among investors who were concerned it could lead to protectionism. However, most have adopted a wait-and-see posture, presuming that Trump's harsh rhetoric is a ploy to negotiate more favorable trade arrangements for the United States.[1]

While Trump's stance is at odds with the traditional Republican adherence to free trade, he is not alone: During the 2016 campaign no Republican candidate defended free trade. Moreover, Hillary Clinton was compelled to withdraw her support for TPP in the face of stinging criticisms from Bernie Sanders. The challenge our political leaders face is they are unsure how to counter accusations that multilateral trade agreements and unfair foreign practices have contributed to the US trade deficits and millions of job losses.

This chapter begins by considering the factors that contributed to a ballooning of the US trade and current account deficits since the early 1980s. The conventional explanation is that it stems from outsized budget deficits that began during the Reagan administration. This is consistent with the data until the mid-1990s. Thereafter, the US budget balance swung from deficit to surplus in the second term of the Clinton administration, but the US current

---

[1] Upon assuming office, President Trump shifted attention to US businesses that have outsourced jobs to workers abroad. His tactic used both the carrot—his pledge to lower the US corporate tax rate to 15%—and the stick—his threat to impose duties on items they import from affiliates abroad. By doing so, the President upped the ante on companies that are planning to locate facilities abroad.

© The Author(s) 2018
N. P. Sargen, *Investing in the Trump Era*,
https://doi.org/10.1007/978-3-319-76045-2_8

account deficit widened steadily, which suggest other forces were at play. The discussion highlights the critical role that international capital flows have played in determining the value of the dollar and the US trade imbalance.

The chapter next considers the extent to which declines in US manufacturing jobs can be linked to the US trade imbalances. We find there is no connection between the US job losses and NAFTA, and that most of the job declines occurred following China's entry into the World Trade Organization (WTO) in 2000. This coincided with a massive buildup in foreign exchange reserves of China and other Asian countries.

The chapter next considers policies that are intended to narrow the United States and global payments imbalances. Unfortunately, the Trump administration's approach of negotiating bilateral trade arrangements will likely prove ineffective, while protectionist measures would invite retaliation. The challenge US policymakers face is how to wean Asian economies away from their export-dependence on the United States without resorting to protectionism that could unsettle financial markets.

The chapter concludes by considering the fate of the US dollar in the Trump era. The dollar initially strengthened after Trump's victory, even though he advocated a weaker dollar on several occasions. However, it surrendered those gains amid a strengthening of the overseas economies and a pause in Fed tightening. While the dollar could regain momentum if US-foreign interest rate differentials were to widen again, the risk of a dollar overshoot such as during the first term of the Reagan administration is low.

Origins of Chronic US Trade Deficits

To understand the impact that international trade may have on the US jobs, it is important to grasp the factors that caused a dramatic shift in the US status from the world's largest creditor nation to its biggest borrower.[2] This transition occurred during the 1980s, and it coincided with the United States running persistent large budget deficits that averaged 3% of GDP during the Reagan and Bush administrations (see Fig. 8.1). Previously, the United States had not run a current account deficit in the post-war era until the 1970s, when oil prices quadrupled on two occasions.

The counterpart of the US shift from a net lender to a borrower was Japan's emergence as the world's largest capital exporter: Japan ran chronic trade surpluses after oil prices plummeted in the early 1980s. This resulted in persistent large bilateral trade imbalances between the United States and Japan that led to policy disputes between the two countries.

---

[2] During the Bretton Woods era of fixed exchange rates from 1944 to 1971, the United States traditionally ran trade and current account surpluses in which exports exceeded imports. These net inflows, in turn, were offset by net capital outflows in the form of net direct investment abroad as US multinationals expanded operations and net US bank lending to banks abroad. As a result, the United States became the world's largest creditor nation.

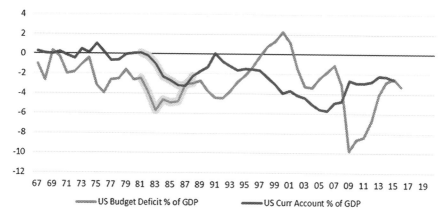

Fig. 8.1 US current account and budget deficits (% of GDP). (Source: Bureau of Economic Analysis, Dept. of Commerce)

According to the Japanese government, the trade imbalances were attributable to lax US fiscal policy that resulted in the United States having "twin deficits." The logic underlying this argument is based on the national income accounting identity:

$$M - X = (G - T) + (I - S).$$

The equation[3] states that a trade imbalance (imports minus exports) is equal to the sum of a budget imbalance (government spending minus tax receipts) and a saving-investment imbalance in the private sector. If the latter imbalance is unchanged, therefore, a change in the budget deficit is associated with a change in the trade imbalance. The intuition is that budget deficits contribute to increased imports but do little to boost exports.

According to this view (which European officials and many prominent US economists also espoused), the best way to reduce the US current account imbalance would be to reduce the budget deficit, either by curtailing spending or by boosting taxes, or a combination of the two. By doing so, aggregate demand would be lower and imports would shrink. Also, a smaller budget deficit would help to reduce bond yields, and thereby cause the dollar to soften as capital inflows from Japan and other countries would moderate.

The US officials at the time countered that the bilateral trade imbalance was mainly the result of the Japan authorities intervening in currency markets to keep the yen undervalued against the dollar. The US government, therefore, pressed the Japanese authorities to refrain from intervening in currency market. Moreover, they pressured the Japanese government to implement "voluntary" export restraints (or quotas) on car shipments to the United States, which it did.

---

[3] This relationship can be derived from two accounting identities, in which GDP is defined as the sum of C+I+G+X−M and also the sum of C+S=T.

Because the US government did not tackle its budget imbalance until the early-1990s, the burden of adjustment for narrowing the trade imbalance was relegated to the yen/dollar exchange rate: It appreciated steadily from 1985 to 1994 and confounded attempts by the Japanese government to counter deflationary pressures that emanated after Japan's real estate and stock market bubble burst. Indeed, in 1993–1994 Treasury Secretary Lloyd Bentsen maintained the yen was undervalued, when it reached a record high of Y80/$—a cumulative appreciation of more than threefold from the beginning of 1980.

Impact of a Global Savings Glut on US Trade

One of the priorities of the Clinton administration was to reverse the direction of US fiscal policy, and it did so through a combination of defense spending cuts and tax rate increases for high-income earners. The economy also proved to be robust during the tech-boom era, when it sustained annualized economic growth of 4%. This helped to generate revenues that brought the federal budget into surplus during the period from fiscal 1998 to 2001, the only surplus years after 1969.

Yet, despite this dramatic improvement in the budgetary picture, the US current account deficit relative to GDP increased steadily from the mid-1990s to the mid-2000s, when it reached a peak of 6% of GDP. A level this high is generally considered to be unsustainable by economists, because it implies a buildup in external debt that is considerably faster than GDP. This forced economists to reassess what was happening, and in 2005 Ben Bernanke, then a Governor of the Federal Reserve, put forth an explanation that the growing US current account deficit was mainly the result of a "global saving glut."[4]

Bernanke's argument is that many of the emerging economies in Asia were devastated by the 1997–1998 crisis, in which their currencies depreciated by record amounts, ranging between nearly 20% for Singapore to more than 70% for Indonesia. This gave them a strong competitive advantage, which enabled them to boost exports while contracting imports. In addition, countries in the region responded by accumulating foreign exchange reserves in the ensuing years to lessen their vulnerability to currency crises in the future. Consequently, they amassed large current account surpluses, mainly with the United States, which in turn experienced a significant rise in its current account deficit.

Roughly one half of the increase in the US current account deficit from 1996 to 2004 was accounted for by China and other emerging Asian economies. Also, if Japan is included along with them, Asian countries accounted for about three-quarters of the increase in the US deficit. Thus, during this period at least the expansion in the US current account deficit was primarily due to an increase in saving outside the United States, rather than due to a deterioration in the US fiscal stance.

[4] Ben S. Bernanke, "The Global Saving Glut and the US Current Account Deficit," Board of Governors of the Federal Reserve, April 14, 2005.

ROLE OF INTERNATIONAL CAPITAL FLOWS

The main takeaway is that international capital flows have been the principal driver of both trade balances and exchange rates since the breakdown of the Bretton Woods system of fixed exchange rates in the early 1970s. According to Robert Aliber, emeritus professor at the University of Chicago's Business School, the key distinction is whether a shortage of US saving "crowded-out" some foreign borrowers from US capital markets or instead whether excess foreign saving "crowded into" the American market and displaced American saving. The conventional view among economists is the former one, but Aliber maintains the latter force has prevailed: "This inflow (of foreign capital) has led to a higher price for the US dollar, a sharp decline in employment in US manufacturing, a US consumption boom, and a larger fiscal deficit."[5]

My own assessment is that both sets of forces have been at play over the past four decades (see Fig. 8.2). The initial bout of chronic US trade imbalances in the 1980s mainly stemmed from the shift to large US budget deficits. When combined with tight monetary policy, they generated record-high real interest rates that induced foreign capital inflows—mainly from Japanese life insurance companies and banks—that caused the dollar to appreciate steadily in the first half of the decade.

Since the mid-1990s, however, the main factor contributing to the increase in the US current account deficit was excess foreign saving, mainly from Asian countries. In this context, much of the capital inflows are the result of direct purchases of US securities by foreign central banks, sovereign wealth funds and government-sponsored entities. A noteworthy example is China, whose holdings of foreign exchange reserves reached a peak of $4 trillion in 2014, largely as a result of purchases of dollar-denominated securities

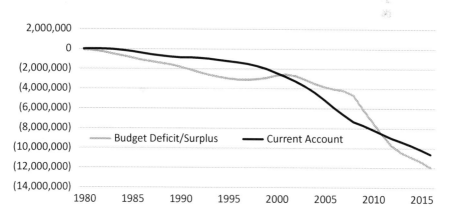

Fig. 8.2 Cumulative US budget and current account deficits, 1980–2017 ($ billions). (Source: US Treasury and Department of Commerce)

[5] Robert Z. Aliber commentary, July 3, 2017.

This experience, in turn, raises the issue of why the adjustment mechanism has not worked as expected in the context of floating exchange rates. The explanation is twofold: First, because the US dollar is the world's key reserve currency, the United States is not subject to the same balance-of-payments constraints that other deficit countries confront. Second, the world's largest surplus countries—mostly in Asia as well as Germany—are not compelled to alter their domestic policies as long as they hold their excess savings in US dollars. Given this predicament, there is no reason for global current account imbalances to change if the respective domestic policies do not change in the United States or the surplus countries.

Job Losses in Manufacturing

We now turn to the issue raised at the outset: Namely, to what extent are US trade deficits linked with job losses in manufacturing? As shown in Fig. 8.3, US manufacturing jobs reached a peak in 1979, and they have since fallen by 7 million to the current level where they stood at the onset of World War II. The initial decline of approximately two million workers occurred in the early 1980s in the context of a super-strong dollar, which created incentives for US multinationals to increase production outside the United States. Thereafter, manufacturing jobs held fairly steady until the 2000–2009 period.

The chart also reveals there is no evidence to support populist rhetoric that NAFTA, which came into play at the beginning of 1994, created significant job losses. In fact, the decade of the 1990s was one of the best periods for job creation in US history, thanks to strong economic growth that accompanied the boom in technology.

Economic studies that have investigated the issue in depth conclude that the effect of NAFTA on the US jobs was marginal. Among the leading experts of trade agreements are Professor Gary Clyde Huffbauer of Georgetown University and Jeffrey J. Schott with the Peterson Institute for International Economics. They wrote a report during the 2008 presidential campaign in response to claims by then Senator Barrack Obama, who cited estimates of one million job losses based on an analysis by union-funded economists.[6] Their response:

> Contrary to the inflated political soundbite of one million jobs lost, the best guess is that NAFTA and other trade agreements have no net effect on the level of employment in the United States or abroad...Moreover, the political soundbite ignores the fact that many American jobs are supported by U.S. merchandise exports to NAFTA partners. Finally the soundbite totally ignores the fact that an integrated and efficient North American economy preserves U.S. production that would otherwise be outsourced to overseas suppliers, in Asia and elsewhere.

[6] Gary Glyde Huffbauer and Jeffrey J. Schott, "NAFTA's Bad Rap," *The International Economy*, Summer 2008.

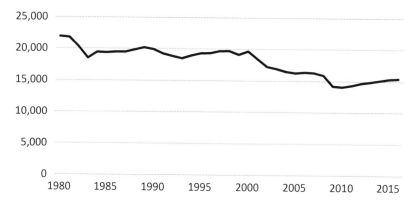

Fig. 8.3 US manufacturing jobs (thousands of persons). (Source: Bureau of Labor and Statistics)

Huffbauer and Schott conclude that NAFTA's bad rap is mainly the result of "sound bites and bumper stickers versus real facts and statistics."

By comparison, there is stronger evidence that US job losses in manufacturing are linked to the widening in the US current account deficit in the past decade, when Asian trade surpluses mushroomed. During this period, US job losses in manufacturing totaled close to five million. The steepest declines occurred in the early part of the decade following China's entry into the WTO and at the end of the decade during the GFC.

It should be noted that this phenomenon is not unique to America: Most industrial countries have experienced job losses in manufacturing, including Germany and Japan, which traditionally have run large trade surpluses (see Fig. 8.4). Consequently, many economists view the decline in manufacturing jobs as an integral part of a transition advanced economies undergo when they shift to become more service sector oriented and knowledge based. The pace of this transition is based on the rate of technological change; consequently, workers who lack technical skills are often the victims.

In the case of Japan, the job losses began with a hollowing out of the country's manufacturing base in the mid-late 1980s. The combination of a strong yen and high wages made it imperative for Japanese companies to relocate operations to other parts of Asia to compete with South Korea, Taiwan and China. Since then, the hollowing-out process has continued fairly steadily, and manufacturing jobs in Japan are now back to their levels at the beginning of the 1960s.

By comparison, Germany has fared better in sustaining its manufacturing base than the United States and Japan. When Germany was unified in the early 1990s, there was a significant rise in unemployment in the former East Germany, because workers were less productive than their counterparts in West Germany and a 1:1 conversion rate was set between the deutsche mark and

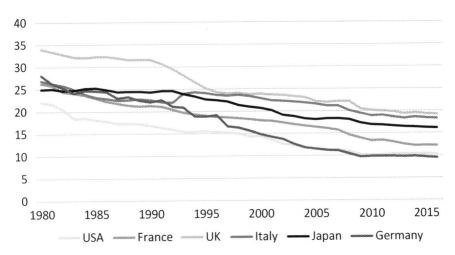

Fig. 8.4 Share of manufacturing in total output for key industrial countries (%). (Source: OECD)

ostmarks. However, conditions eventually stabilized, and the German economy benefitted from labor market reforms that were undertaken in the mid-2000s, which introduced greater wage flexibility into the system. In addition, Germany's reliance on small- and mid-sized firms and its unique system of on-the-job training has enabled it to meet the challenge from foreign competition.

The main takeaway from this comparison is that while advanced countries have become more service-oriented and knowledge-based as they develop, some have done a better job at sustaining manufacturing jobs. The key to success is having flexible labor markets and on-the-job training programs.

Policies to Tackle Payments Imbalances

While the link between job losses and trade deficits is ambiguous, there is widespread agreement among economists and policymakers that the US current account deficit and surpluses in Asia and Germany are too large. One concern is they could be destabilizing if they were to result in rapid debt accumulation by deficit countries. Another concern is they may contribute to protectionism. Therefore, it is important to consider what policies should be pursued to narrow global payments imbalances that will not unsettle financial markets.

The approach the Trump administration is pursuing focuses on bilateral trade balances. Thus, the Department of Commerce under Secretary Wilbur Ross is earmarking countries with the largest bilateral trade imbalances with the United States, and it then disaggregates the imbalances further on product-by-product basis. The intent is to pressure surplus countries into reducing their exports to the United States or to increase their imports.

The problem with this approach is that it fails to consider the macro forces at play that are the critical drivers of trade imbalances and exchange rates. Two prominent economists and former policymakers, George Shultz and Martin Feldstein, state the flaws with the administration's approach as follows[7]:

> If a country consumes more than it produces, it must import more than it exports. That's not a rip-off; that's arithmetic. If we manage to negotiate a reduction in the Chinese trade surplus with the United States, we will have an increased trade deficit with some other country.

> Federal deficit spending, a massive and continuous act of dissaving is the culprit. Control that spending and you will control trade deficits.

The argument that Shultz and Feldstein advance in essence is the "twin deficit" view that was discussed previously. It is sound advice, as it rightly concludes the United States will continue to run large trade deficits as long as the federal budget deficit remains large. One way the Trump administration could lower the trade deficit would be to reduce the size of the budget deficit, but prospective tax cuts if anything are likely to increase it.

Beyond this, it is also relevant to consider what can be done to encourage surplus countries to increase domestic spending. This has proved to be a challenge throughout the period of flexible exchange rates. In the 1980s, for example, the US government conceived a "locomotive strategy" in which the leading surplus countries—Japan and Germany—would boost government spending to stimulate economic growth. When this did not materialize, the US government subsequently pressured Japan to restrain its exports to the United States and to allow the yen to appreciate steadily. Yet, the huge appreciation of the yen during the 1980s and 1990s had little effect on Japan's current account surplus.

The situation today is equally daunting, with China and emerging Asian economies also running persistent large surpluses. These countries followed Japan's example and based their development strategies on promoting strong export growth, as American consumers became hooked on cheap imports. In their book, *Currency Conflict and Trade Policy*, Fred Bergsten and Joseph Gagnon refer to the period from 2003 to 2013 as "The Decade of Manipulation" to describe a decade of unprecedented foreign exchange intervention.[8] They estimate that during this period net official capital flows averaged more than $1 trillion annually, more than half of which they consider to be excessive.

Since the mid-2000s that US policymakers have pressed the Chinese authorities to refrain from purchasing dollars to keep the yuan artificially cheap, and Chinese foreign exchange reserves have fallen by about $1 trillion in recent

---

[7] George P. Shultz and Martin Feldstein, "Everything you need to know about trade economics in 70 words," *Washington Post*, May 5, 2017.

[8] See C. Fred Bergsten and Joseph E. Gagnon, *Currency Conflict and Trade Policy—A New Strategy for the United States*, Peterson Institute for International Economics, June 2017.

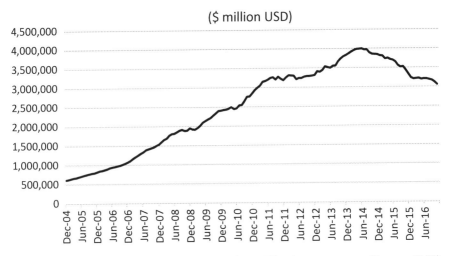

($ million USD)

Fig. 8.5 China's foreign exchange reserves have fallen in recent years. (Source: IMF)

years (Fig. 8.5). This suggests the authorities have acted to limit the depreciation of the yuan against the dollar. Consequently, the argument that China is manipulating its currency to weaken it no longer applies, and the Trump administration has not brought trade sanctions against China. The main reason is it is hoping the Chinese government will use its influence on North Korea to lessen geopolitical tensions. However, the administration could change its stance at any time if it deems the Chinese government is not doing enough to restrain the government of North Korea. Consequently, the potential for protectionism and retaliation remains a risk to the outlook.

One proposal by Bergsten and Gannon that would lessen the risk is to have the US government state it is prepared to purchase currencies of countries that accumulate excess dollar reserves as a way to deter them[9]:

> We have already suggested that the most effective policy response to the risk of future currency aggression would be the announcement by the United States that it would henceforth carry out countervailing currency intervention against any G-20 country that met the relevant criteria and sought to prevent appreciation of its exchange rate by intervening directly in the foreign exchange markets...

> Unlike countervailing duties or other trade policy sanctions that apply only to imports, the new policy would address both sides of the trade equation.

PROSPECTS FOR THE US DOLLAR

Finally, we consider the implications of these issues for the US dollar. Immediately following Trump's election win, the US unit surged against most currencies, as market participants anticipated stronger growth would cause US

[9] IBID, p. 187.

interest rates to rise. By early 2017, the dollar stood at a 14-year high on a trade-weighted basis, which posed a challenge for the Trump administration's goal of narrowing the trade imbalance. President Trump, in turn, responded by reiterating his campaign declaration that the US currency was too strong.

The dollar subsequently gave ground against most currencies and went on to surrender all of its gains since the November election. However, President Trump's declarations were not the primary cause. Rather, the main factor was that investors revised their forecasts for growth abroad upward, especially for the eurozone and Asia. At the same time, political risks in the eurozone lessened as populist candidates lost elections in France, Holland and Germany.

Looking ahead, the prospects for the dollar will be influenced, to a large extent, by monetary policies in the United States and abroad and by US-foreign interest rate differentials. The strengthening of the dollar from mid-2014 to early 2017 coincided with the Federal Reserve phasing down its QE program and raising short-term interest rates, while central banks in Europe and Japan kept interest rates at or below zero. The case for a stronger dollar is that the Fed is now scaling back its balance sheet gradually and interest rates are set to rise further, whereas the ECB and BOJ have yet to normalize their monetary policies.

One outcome that I had considered shortly after the presidential election was the possibility the dollar could overshoot its long-term equilibrium value considerably, as it did during the first term of the Reagan administration. My reasoning was that the Trump administration appeared to be pursuing fiscal policies similar to Reagan's, which would cause the budget deficit to blow out, while the Fed would be compelled to raise interest rates to offset this development. However, in the wake of the debate over tax cuts and the budget, this risk has lessened, as it is clear Congressional Republicans are opposed to a major expansion in the budget deficit. Therefore, it is unlikely real interest rates will rise as much as they did during the first half of the 1980s.

Finally, one must also recognize there is a considerable difference between Ronald Reagan's view that a strong dollar was an important symbol of America's resurgence and Donald Trump's view that a strong dollar hurts American workers. Reagan's pro-dollar stance helped to attract capital inflows into the United States at a time when inflation stood at record levels, and the administration did not alter its stance until 1985, when there was clear evidence the strong dollar was undermining US growth. By comparison, President Trump's stance on both the US trade and the dollar runs the risk that it could undermine investor confidence if US growth were to falter. If so, capital flight from the United States could occur that would adversely impact both the stock and bond markets.

APPENDIX: REVISITING THE CASE FOR FREE TRADE

As students of economics know, the argument in favor of free trade is among the oldest theories in economics, dating back to the late eighteenth century and the works of David Hume, Adam Smith and David Ricardo. Prior to their writings, the prevailing economic doctrine was mercantilism, which equated economic strength with trade surpluses and economic weakness with trade deficits. The logic was that countries that ran trade surpluses accumulated gold, which enabled them to acquire wealth and power. However, Hume subsequently articulated the price-specie flow mechanism to show that countries which acquired gold would see their money supplies increase, which would boost prices and thereby make them less competitive. As a result, they would be unable to sustain trade surpluses indefinitely.

Adam Smith's contribution was to demonstrate that free trade, or open exchange of goods and services, was beneficial to society because it fostered division of labor and economies of scale in production. The intuition is that people are better off specializing in what they produce than if they tried to produce everything by themselves. Also, the presumption is that two parties would not enter into an exchange voluntarily unless they believed they would be better off. Note that this is very different from Trump's perspective in which there are winners (surplus countries) and losers (deficit countries) from trade.

David Ricardo subsequently took the argument a step farther by distinguishing between absolute and comparative advantage. The law of comparative advantage states that countries will maximize their wealth if they specialize in what they are most efficient in producing and then trade surplus products with other countries that are *relatively* more efficient in producing other products. Thus, even if a country is more productive in producing many types of goods than other countries, it is still advantageous for it to concentrate production where it has a comparative advantage.

By and large, the principles of free trade carried the day during the nineteenth century and into the twentieth century until the Great Depression, when commodity prices plummeted and countries were forced off of the gold standard. In the wake of this, many countries pursued beggar-my-neighbor policies, in which they erected tariff barriers to protect domestic industries while also depreciating their currencies to gain a competitive advantage.

During the post-war era, the overarching goal of policymakers in the United States and other advanced economies was to reestablish free trade and to restore currency convertibility. For most economists, this commitment was a key component behind the revival of many economies from the devastation of the war.

Some developing countries, however, questioned whether free trade was beneficial for them, and they maintained that free trade was not the same as fair trade. One of their complaints was that while developed countries lowered tariffs on high value-added products, they continued to protect their agricultural sectors (especially in the EU), which makes it more difficult for primary-producing countries to penetrate. Another objection is that whereas advanced countries specialize in and dominate high-tech sectors and specialized manufacturing, which command high and stable prices, developing countries are relegated to specialize in low value-added products, which have little pricing power.

Consequently, many countries in Latin America sought to overcome this perceived disadvantage by pursuing import substitution strategies, in which domestic industries were protected by high tariffs. However, by the latter part of the twentieth century it had become clear that most Asian economies, which pursued export-oriented strategies, had far outperformed their Latin counterparts, and many Latin American countries concluded they needed to do the same.

PART IV

Globalization and Financial Markets

CHAPTER 9

Globalization and Widening Income Inequality

Globalization—the increased integration of the world's economies via international trade and ready movement of capital, labor and technology across national boundaries—was widely seen as positive development throughout the second half of the twentieth century. It enabled Europe and Japan to rebuild their war-ravished economies, and it helped transform emerging economies following the collapse of the Soviet Union. The US economy, in turn, benefited from robust growth abroad, and along with rapid technological change, it attained a growth of 4% per annum in the second half of the 1990s.

Since then, however, several developments have caused some observers to look at globalization in a less favorable light. One is the sluggish pace of economic activity that has ensued following the bursting of the tech and housing bubbles. Another is the threat of terrorism that the tragedy of 9/11 highlighted and which has increased amid instability in the Middle East. During 2016–2017, policies toward immigration emerged as important issues in the referendum over Brexit and during election campaigns in the United States, Austria, Holland, France and Germany.

Within the United States, there is growing recognition today that globalization has been a factor contributing to increased income disparities. Thus, while highly educated workers have benefited from expanded opportunities internationally, less educated workers have been displaced by competition and/or suffered declines in real incomes as wages stagnated. This has given rise to a perception that globalization has contributed to a widening divide between "The Haves" and "The Have Nots."

This chapter investigates the impact of globalization on income and employment in the United States, as well as policies that can be pursued to lessen the divide. Many economists favor policies to increase educational attainment for young people, on grounds that returns on investment in human capital are high. Others favor increased taxes on the very wealthy (top one percentile) as

© The Author(s) 2018
N. P. Sargen, *Investing in the Trump Era*,
https://doi.org/10.1007/978-3-319-76045-2_9

a way to narrow income disparities, although research on this issue suggests the effects may be minimal. Also, while Germany's program of apprenticeships has been very successful, it is not easy to transfer it to America.

The broader issue the United States and other countries face is how to capture the benefits of increased access to foreign economies and markets, while lessening the adverse consequences for low-skilled workers. One approach is to turn inward by erecting barriers to the flow of trade, capital, labor and technology. However, countries that have pursued such an approach have underperformed more-open economies.

Finally, while globalization has contributed to a declining share of labor income, the counterpart—rising US corporate profit margins—has helped to buoy the US stock market. Attempts to roll back globalization by pursuing nationalist policies, therefore, could undermine the stock market.

Changing Perceptions of Globalization

One of the most powerful forces after World War II has been the increasing integration of the world economy via flows of trade, capital, labor and technology. This was no accident. It was governed by a set of arrangements that Western governments adopted at the Bretton Woods conference in 1944 under US–UK leadership. The overriding objectives were (i) to create a system of fixed exchange rates that would foster low inflation and free trade and (ii) to ensure the system was also sufficiently flexible to foster long-term economic growth and development. They were a response to developments during the Great Depression, in which countries were forced off the gold standard, and competitive depreciations ensued along with increased barriers to trade and capital flows.

While the system of fixed exchange rates ultimately broke down in the early 1970s, when the United States became a high-inflation country, it did not disrupt the process of economic integration. Western countries reduced tariffs and other trade barriers steadily under the auspices of the General Agreement on Tariffs and Trade (GATT), and beginning in the 1980s they embarked on a series of policy actions to liberalize capital controls and to deregulate their domestic financial systems. During the 1990s, the breakdown of the Soviet Union and Eastern bloc created impetus for emerging economies to pursue market-oriented strategies, although the ensuing Asian Financial Crisis caused policymakers in Asia to challenge the so-called Washington consensus that posited the virtues of these strategies.[1]

Throughout this period, policymakers in the United States believed the effects of globalization were generally positive for the US economy, and that its impact on wealth and jobs were largely benign. However, as Nobel Laureate

---

[1] The Washington consensus is a set of policy prescriptions that are typically recommended by institutions such as the IMF, World Bank and US Treasury Department. The prescriptions include stabilization measures to lessen inflation, opening of international trade and capital flows, and liberalization of domestic financial markets, among others.

economist Michael Spence observes, perceptions began to change around the turn of this century, as emerging economies moved up the value-added chain and began to compete directly with advanced economies[2]:

> The major emerging economies are becoming more competitive in areas in which the U.S. economy has historically been dominant, such as the design and manufacture of semi-conductors, pharmaceuticals, and information technology devices.
>
> At the same time, many job opportunities in the United States are shifting away from the sectors that are experiencing the most growth and to those that are experiencing less. The result is growing disparities in income and employment across the U.S. economy, with highly educated workers enjoying more opportunities and workers with less education facing declining employment prospects and stagnant incomes.

In a Foreign Affairs article written in 2011, Spence notes that since 1990 the employment structure of the US economy has been shifting away from the tradable sector: 98% of the 27 million jobs created between 1990 and 2008 were in the nontraded goods sector, and of these two sectors—government and healthcare—accounted for 40% of the new jobs.[3] Spence also points out that over this same period value-added per employee in the traded goods sector (where jobs growth has been slow) increased by 52% compared with just 12% in the nontraded goods sector. The implication is that highly educated workers who found jobs in the traded goods sector (which includes financial services) were able to reap substantially larger income gains than those who are less skilled and who work in the nontraded goods sector.

Declining Share of Labor Income

One phenomenon that has accompanied globalization in the past two decades has been a decline in the share of wage income in national income. This share fluctuated in a narrow band centered at about 63% of national income for most of the post-war period. However, it has declined to about 57–58% in the past 15 years or so (see Fig. 9.1). When proprietors' income is included along with wages, the respective decline is from 73% to 69%.

Moreover, as Kim Schoenholtz of NYU observes, the decline in the share of labor income is a global phenomenon. Thus, according to the Penn World Table, in 95 of 130 countries, the latest reported labor share was below the average that prevailed until 2000. On average, the latest observation is 2.8 percentage points below the pre-2000 average.[4]

[2] Michael Spence, "The Impact of Globalization on Income and Employment," *Foreign Affairs*, July/August 2011.

[3] Ibid., p. 30.

[4] Kim Schoenholtz commentary, "Labor's Declining Share: A Primer," June 5, 2017.

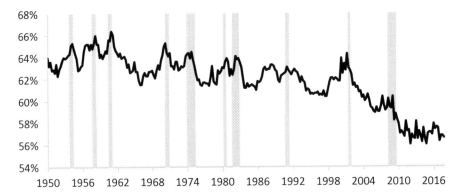

Fig. 9.1 US labor's share of national income, 1947-1Q2017. (Source: U.S. Bureau of Labor Statistics)

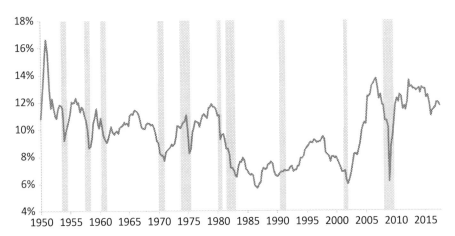

Fig. 9.2 US corporate profits as a share of national income, 1947-1Q2017. (Corporate profits before tax and without IVA and CCAdj. Source: U.S. Bureau of Economic Analysis)

Economists at the IMF are now exploring what is causing this phenomenon.[5] One possibility is that technological advances have lowered the price of capital goods relative to labor, which have encouraged businesses to substitute capital for labor. Another explanation is that there has been a deepening in global value chains, which usually involve shifting from local production that is labor intensive to production abroad that deploys cheaper labor. An additional consideration is that globalization has contributed to "super-star" firms with global brands, and they are able to attain economies of scale as their industry concentration rises.

The counterpart to this trend is that the share of corporate profits to national income has increased considerably in the past two decades (Fig. 9.2). This development has enabled the US stock market to set record highs, as businesses have

[5] IMF, *World Economic Outlook*, Chapter 3, April 2017.

adapted to an environment of lower economic growth by expanding their profit margins. Nonetheless, while outsized stock market returns have increased wealth of shareholders, the vast majority of wage earners have not participated, which has skewed income and wealth distribution in America since the GFC.

US Income Distribution Becomes More Skewed

During the period from World War II until the 1970s, prosperity in America was widely shared across all income classes. However, income inequality in the United States has increased steadily over the past four decades. According to CBO data as of 2013 (the latest available), the top quintile of US households experienced an increase of 86% in inflation-adjusted pre-tax income from 1979, more than two times above the increases for those in the four lower quintiles. This outcome has increased the share of US income for the top quintile relative to the other four quintiles, each of whose share has declined (Fig. 9.3).[6] Moreover, the gap is considerably wider for the top percentile, whose pre-tax income rose on average by 187%. According to research by Emmanuel Saez of UC-Berkeley, the US income inequality has now reached levels not seen since the "Gilded Age" of the 1920s.[7]

US inequality also stands out when compared with other advanced countries. Among the main findings of the Stanford Center on Poverty and Inequality in its *2016 Annual Report* are the United States has unusually high levels of income and wealth inequality, and it also has unusually high levels of poverty.[8] These findings are not surprising considering the welfare state in Europe is more extensive than in America. However, they also apply when comparing the United States with other Anglo-Saxon countries such as the United Kingdom, Canada, Australia and New Zealand.

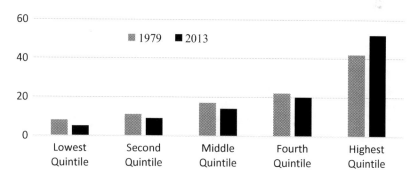

Fig. 9.3   US income by income group, percent change 1979–2013. (Source: CBO)

[6] CBO, "The Distribution of Household Income and Federal Taxes, 2013" Supplemental Data
[7] Drew Desilver, Pew Research Center, "U.S. income inequality, on the rise for decades, is now the highest since 1928."
[8] Stanford Center on Poverty and Inequality, *State of the Union, 2016.*

Among the more surprising findings of the Stanford Center report is that the United States scores poorly in domains that have historically been regarded as it strengths. The stylized story is that however unequal its income distribution may be, it is a land of opportunity where everyone has a legitimate shot at getting ahead. However, the report finds the opposite to be true:

> The data presented in Ch. 7 indicate that in fact the birth lottery matters *more* in the U.S. than in most well-off countries. The intergenerational earnings elasticity, which speaks to the pay-off that accrues to being born into higher-earning families, is substantially larger in the U.S. than in many countries that are not routinely featured as the 'land of opportunity.'[9]

One of the silver linings in the Stanford study is that although the United States has a higher rate of poverty than other advanced countries, it is mainly due to a lower safety net rather than to economic performance. The study concludes that this is good news for the following reason:

> It is much easier to ramp up the safety net than to revamp the economy and labor market in ways that deliver higher market incomes. If you have to choose your problem, it is far better in this sense to have a political problem (ie. an underperforming safety net) than an economic one (ie. an underperforming economy.)[10]

These findings are consistent with those of Harvard University's Equality of Opportunity Project, which found that upward mobility in the United States is not uniform, and that some regions of the country consistently offer less economic mobility.[11] Also, while the report found that income mobility has been

Weighing Equality Versus Efficiency
One of the objectives of this book is to assess how economic policies currently being considered will impact financial markets. By doing so, we can establish an objective standard for the reader to assess whether the policy assessments in the book represent sound investment advice. At the same time, one must be cognizant that policies that elicit favorable market responses may not always represent good public policy. The reason: Markets invariably favor policies that investors deem to offer improved allocative efficiency (and/or which favor them) versus policies that redistribute income from the wealthy to the less wealthy.

For the most part, the economics profession does not get embroiled in discussions that weigh the trade-off between equality and efficiency. The

(*continued*)

[9] Ibid.
[10] Ibid.
[11] Steven J. Markovich, Council on Foreign Relations, "The Income Inequality Debate," February 3, 2014

(continued)

primary reason is the choice ultimately involves making value judgments that the economics profession wishes to avoid in order to maintain a scientific standard of analysis. The reality, however, is that economists who engage in debates over public policy issues invariably wind up making such value judgments.

One of the best discussions of this issue is contained in a book written by Arthur Okun in 1975 titled *Equality and Efficiency: The Big Tradeoff.*[12] Okun begins his analysis by observing there is a double standard in American society, which on one hand proclaims the worth of every human being and professes an egalitarian political and social system, while on the other hand generates gaping disparities in income levels. He observes that the US constitution bestows a number of entitlements and privileges for all citizens, but the marketplace assigns rights to purchase items that are bought and sold for dollars. Okun then considers how and where society draws the boundary lines between the domain of social rights and that of the marketplace.

The thrust of Okun's analysis is that both equality and efficiency are valued, and policymakers should strive to find compromises when the two goals are in conflict. The real issue is one of degree. He observes the standard textbook answer is policymakers should promote equality up to where the added benefits are just matched by the added costs of greater inefficiency. However, Okun goes on to point out how difficult this is to achieve in practice, and he observes "decision makers do not get opportunities in the real world to test neatly their priorities between the two competing claims." Further complicating matters is the issue of "leaky buckets" or inefficiencies of real-world redistribution that arise from the administrative costs of tax collection and transfer programs.

Okun concludes with the following assessment:

> The fulfillment of the right to survival and the eradication of poverty are within the grasp of this affluent nation. And within our vision is the target of half of average income as the basic minimum...
>
> I have stressed particularly the urgency of assisting the bottom fifth on the income scale and helping them into the mainstream of our affluent society. I believe that programs to help them rise would generate momentum through time and into wider ranges of the income distribution.

Finally, it should be noted that when Okun wrote his book in 1975, the distribution of income in the United States was relatively unchanged since the end of World War II. As noted in this chapter, US income distribution has become much more unequal in the meantime, with the share going to the top 1% rising from about 8% of income in the late 1970s to about 20% currently. In this respect, the problem of inequality is much greater today than any time since the 1920s.

---

[12] Arthur M. Okun, Equality and Efficiency: The Big Tradeoff, The Brookings Institution, Washington, D.C. 1975.

stable across quintiles, income inequality is growing in an absolute sense, as the gaps between median incomes in each quintile have grown. A Brookings Institution study found that 47% of US parents' income advantages are passed on to their children, which is the second highest rate among advanced economies.

POLICIES TO ADDRESS GROWING INCOME INEQUALITY

Amid growing recognition of the plight of the US worker, what can be done to mitigate the problem of widening disparities in income and wealth?

One way conceivably would be to reverse the decline in unionization that has accompanied globalization, as the median union member earns roughly a quarter more than a nonunion counterpart. Forty years ago, for example, one-quarter of private sector workers belonged to a labor union, compared with 7% today. Nobel Laureate economist Paul Krugman of Princeton has argued that "we need to restore the bargaining power that labor has lost over the last thirty years, so that ordinary workers as well as superstars have the power to bargain for good wages."[13] Implicit in this argument, however, is the businesses that employ these workers must have greater protection from foreign competition. The problem with the argument for increased unionization, in short, is that it ignores what is causing the problem!

The route that many economists favor is to improve the education of American workers. Nobel Laureate economist Gary Becker and Kevin Murphy contend that educational attainment is a major driver of rising income inequality, and they believe returns on investment in human capital are beneficial and desirable.[14] In a report published by the American Enterprise Institute (AEI), they illustrate how higher educational attainment—both undergraduate and graduate—has translated into an increasing wage premium over time when compared with high school graduates. For example, in 1980 an American with a college degree earned about 30% more than one with a high school education, whereas in the mid-2000s a person with a college degree earned roughly 70% more (Fig. 9.4).

Becker and Murphy go on to argue that the potential generated by higher returns to education extends from individuals to the economy as a whole. It shows up as a source of rising wages, productivity and living standards, as well as providing a wide range of benefits not captured by GDP. From this perspective, the higher rates of return on education are a positive outcome, even though it is a source of wider income disparity.

At the same time, Becker and Murphy share concerns that not enough high school graduates go on to college and that a high proportion of American youth drop out of high school, especially African American and Hispanic males. In their view, this is mainly attributable to the breakdown in the American family and the resulting low skill levels acquired by many children from broken households. The report concludes:

[13] Ibid., p. 5.
[14] Gary Becker and Kevin M. Murphy, AEI, "The Upside of Income Inequality," May 7, 2007.

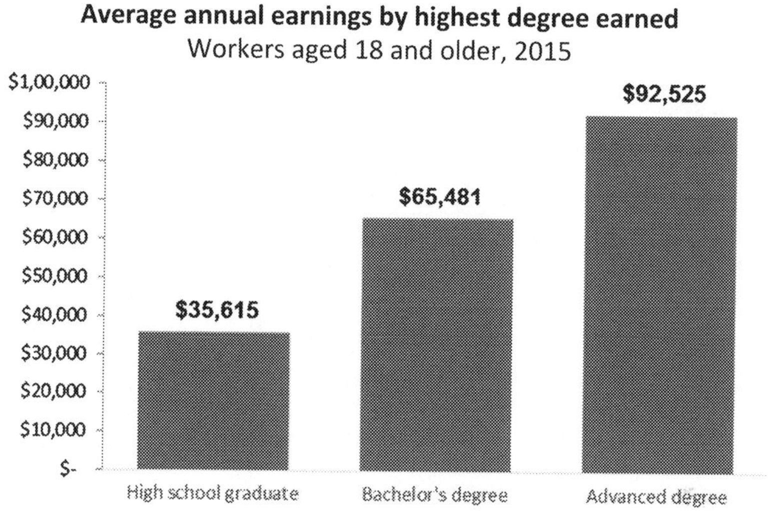

Average annual earnings by highest degree earned
Workers aged 18 and older, 2015

Fig. 9.4   Educational attainment and income levels. (Source: Census Bureau, JP Morgan)

So instead of lamenting the increased earnings gap caused by education, policymakers and the public should focus attention on how to raise the fraction of American youth who complete high school and then go on for a college education. Solutions are not cheap or easy. But it will be a disaster if the focus remains so much on the earnings inequality itself that Congress tries to interfere directly with this inequality rather than trying to raise the educational levels of those left behind.[15]

One counterargument to this assessment is that US income inequality is high relative to other advanced countries, in part, because personal taxes are relatively low. According to OECD data, taxes and social security contributions as a share of GDP are more than ten percentage points below the unweighted average of 21 other industrial countries, with only Ireland having a lower tax rate.[16] Therefore, some observers contend it is imperative to make the tax code more progressive, by raising taxes on the wealthiest in order to address the problem of income inequality.

It is questionable, however, whether such a policy stance would be effective. For example, a study by economists at the Brookings Institution conducted a simulation analysis to determine how much of a reduction in income inequality would be achieved from increasing the top individual tax rate to as much as 50%.[17] The study assumed an explicit redistribution of additional revenues

[15] Ibid., p. 5.

[16] Martin H. Barnes, BCA Research, "U.S. Fiscal Policy: Facts, Fallacies and Fantasies," April 5, 2017.

[17] William G. Gale, Melissa S. Kearney, and Peter R. Orzag, Brooking Institution Economic Studies, "Would a significant increase in the top income tax rate substantially alter income inequality." September 2015.

would accrue to households in the bottom quintile of income distribution. The report concludes that "the resulting effects on overall income inequality are exceedingly modest."

Yet another approach would be to tackle low educational attainment and low jobs skills more directly by improving the quality of education. For its part, the Trump administration, with Betsy DeVos as education secretary, has favored increased use of charter schools in low-income areas. Advocates of charter schools contend they offer families greater choice in selecting schools, and they have more flexible and innovative curriculums than traditional schools. Yet, charter schools are often opposed by school administrators and teachers unions, because they don't have to follow the rules in a public school district, and they often do not hire unionized teachers. Nonetheless, the growing appeal of charter schools is evident in the number of attendees, which doubled from 2008 to 2014, reaching 2.5 million students, or 5% of total attendees.

Finally, another approach that is being considered would increase on-the-job training and vocational schools so that workers can develop the necessary skills to be productive in a world of rapid technological change. In this regard, Germany's apprenticeship model stands out as an effective way to teach young people a professional trade, and it has enabled Germany to retain a higher share of workers in manufacturing than most other advanced countries. Whereas in America today fewer than 5% of young people serve as apprentices, the number in Germany is closer to 60%.[18] The German program is called "dual training," because trainees split their days between classroom instruction at a vocational school and on-the-job training at a company.

Nonetheless, while the benefits of Germany's apprentice program are readily apparent, there are several factors that make it challenging to adopt in the United States. They include the following: (i) Costs of the program are high, ranging from $25,000 to $80,000 per apprentice, and would likely be more costly in America; (ii) the German system is highly centralized and the state plays an important role in overseeing what happens in private companies and (iii) American attitudes view such programs as "blue collar," and it is more prestigious to have a college degree than a technical degree.[19] Consequently, while many economists favor government-sponsored programs to help train workers that have lost their jobs, there are numerous challenges to implement programs that will be effective.

The good news from all this is there is now growing recognition that widening income and wealth disparity is a problem that needs to be addressed. However, there are no quick and easy solutions. The key is to focus efforts on improving the quality of education so American workers can compete in a global market place that is subject to rapid technological change.

---

[18] Tamar Jacoby, *The Atlantic*, "Why Germany is So Much Better at Training Its Workers," October 16, 2014.
[19] Ibid.

DEVELOPMENT STRATEGIES

At a macro level, the United States and other countries must ultimately decide whether to remain open to international trade and capital flows or to turn inward and pursue protectionist policies. There have been varied responses throughout the post-war era, but the historical record is unambiguous: Countries that have embraced the need to compete internationally have substantially outperformed those that have not.

Latin American countries, for example, initially rejected free trade principles, as policymakers in the region pursued import-substitution strategies, in which high tariff barriers were erected to subsidize infant industries. However, many of these industries were inefficient and unable to compete internationally. During the developing country debt crisis in the 1980s, Western governments pressed the debtor countries to undertake market-oriented reforms to make them more competitive, which enabled them to regain access to international credit markets. Also, following the collapse of the Soviet Union in the early 1990s, former Eastern bloc countries transformed their economies so they could compete internationally.

This does not mean the choice is always easy. As noted previously, countries in Asia experienced massive capital flight during the second half of the 1990s, and many questioned the "Washington consensus" that advocated free movement of capital and financial market liberalization. Moreover, the fallout from the GFC reinforced their reluctance to follow the lead of Western countries. That said, Asian countries have continued to pursue their export-oriented development strategies.

Since the GFC, the spotlight has turned to the EU and eurozone, as highly indebted countries were compelled to pursue austerity policies to gain necessary funding from creditor countries. One year after a bailout package was negotiated with Greece to enable it to remain in the eurozone, the British electorate voted to opt out of the EU. Proponents of Brexit are quick to point out that the United Kingdom has not experienced dire consequences—recession and rising unemployment—that opponents claimed would ensue. However, the process of withdrawing membership from the EU will take two years, and it is too early to assess what the costs will be.

In the wake of President Trump's election, many observers concluded that the era of globalization was coming to an end. This conclusion, however, is premature, as subsequent elections in Holland, France and Germany resulted in populist candidates being rejected. The most significant was Emmanuel Macron's election as France's president and the ability of his newly formed party to win a majority in parliament. Macron is now committed to embark on comprehensive reforms of France's antiquated labor laws, which have undermined the country's competitiveness. In Germany's case, structural reforms of its labor market provided a catalyst for the country to reduce unemployment from high levels, and the same could apply to France and other countries that move in this direction.

The bottom line is that the most successful countries are ones that are able to adapt to a rapidly changing conditions in the global economy. Those that are unable to undertake necessary structural reforms have fallen further behind.

INVESTMENT IMPLICATIONS: GLOBALIZATION AND THE US STOCK MARKET

While the impact of globalization on the US economy has been mixed, its overall impact on the US stock market has been unambiguously positive since the mid-1990s: The stock market has quadrupled in value since then, even though it experienced declines of 50% following the bursting of the tech bubble and again during the GFC. In report written in the first quarter of 2017, Jeremy Grantham of GMO points out three ways in which stock market trends in the past 20 years have shifted from their averages in 1970–1996[20]:

- First, the average P/E multiple has risen to more than 23 times earnings from 14 times. Moreover, following the bursting of the tech bubble the multiple did not decline to its former trend at any point, and after the onset of the GFC it only fell below the prior trend for a six-month period.
- Second, the share of after-tax corporate profits (measured as a percent of nonfinancial corporate profits relative to GDP) has risen to 4.5% from 3.8% previously. The 30% shift in corporate margins represents a large and sustained change.
- Third, real interest rates, in the past 20 years have been the lowest in history. This development impacts valuations, as real interest rates are the basis used to discount future cash flows.

Both the rise in the share of corporate profits to GDP and the decline in real interest rates, in turn, are directly linked to globalization. They are both counterparts to the decline in the share of labor income that was discussed previously. Stated differently, globalization effectively has increased the pool of workers available to businesses, which has put downward pressure on wages and interest rates, and in turn, has elevated corporate profits relative to the prior trend.

Beyond this, Grantham maintains that globalization has also had an impact on boosting the franchise value (or brand value) of multinational businesses[21]:

Increased globalization has no doubt increased the value of brands, and the US has much more than its fair share of both the old established brands of the Coca-Cola and J&J variety and the new ones like Apple, Amazon, and Facebook. Even much more domestic brands – wakeboard distributors would be a suitable example – have allowed for returns on required capital to handsomely improve by moving capital to handsomely improve by moving the capital-intensive production to China and retaining only the brand management in the US.

[20] Jeremy Grantham, GMO Quarterly Letter, "This Time Seems Very, Very Different," 1Q2017.
[21] Ibid., p. 12.

One, of course, may ask why unusually high-profit margins have not been bid away by new entrants. Grantham's explanation is that there has been a steady decline in new entrants into the US business world since the mid-1980s. His explanation is that increased regulations cost businesses money, but the largest ones are better suited to absorb these costs than small- or mid-size companies: Thus regulations, however necessary to the well-being of ordinary people, are in the aggregate anti-competitive. They form a protective moat for large, established firms.[22]

---

[22] Ibid, p. 13.

CHAPTER 10

Economic and Market Prospects for the Medium Term

As I've mentioned, my purpose in writing this book is to provide investors and voters alike with a context to understand key policy issues that surfaced during the 2016 presidential election and that will likely influence future elections. In previous chapters we showed how the respective issues have evolved over time, what the current debates are and how they are impacting various market segments. In this concluding chapter, we assess how policies under consideration are likely to impact the economy and financial markets during the remainder of the Trump era.

Following Donald Trump's surprise victory, equities and other risk assets surged as investors were buoyed by his pro-growth message and the prospect of an end to political gridlock. One challenge they confronted was to assess whether the White House or Republican Congressional leaders would call the shots on policy changes, especially pertaining to corporate and personal taxes. The President's predilection for making off-the-cuff statements and tweets added to uncertainty. Accordingly, my message for investors was to stay focused on legislation that would be enacted.

The biggest surprise was that no major policy legislation was enacted until December, even though Republicans controlled both houses of Congress. Failure to repeal and replace Obamacare, however, did not deter the stock market from setting record highs, and volatility plummeted despite the political rancor in Washington, DC, and heightened geopolitical tensions.

Nonetheless, as the second year of President Trump's term began, investors were wondering how long this dichotomy would last. My take was passage of corporate tax reform—the "holy grail" for President Trump and the Republican Party—was the most important policy issue for investors, and I offered the following assessment of prospects for the economy and markets for 2018 and beyond following its passage.

© The Author(s) 2018
N. P. Sargen, *Investing in the Trump Era*,
https://doi.org/10.1007/978-3-319-76045-2_10

Cyclical Developments Will Bolster the Economy and Financial Markets in the Near Term The US and overseas economies are experiencing the first synchronized expansion since 2010, and 2018 could be the year in which US economic growth breaks out of the 2% doldrums. Also, while the Federal Reserve began to shrink its balance sheet and other central banks may follow suit, interest rates are unlikely to spike as long as inflation stays tame.

Secular Forces, Nonetheless, Will Make It Difficult to Restore Growth to Its Former Trend of 3% per Annum Notably, growth of labor supply and productivity will continue to be a drag on the economy, and prospective corporate and personal tax cuts will provide only a partial offset. Growth in coming years at best will average 2.2–2.5% per annum.

Budget Matters Will Take on Added Importance in the Next Few Years The reason: The number of retirees is growing, which increases the burden for entitlement programs. The tax legislation that was enacted was a combination of reforms and stimulus, and the latter will add to the future debt burden.

Policies That Lessen Regulatory Burdens Should Give Smaller Businesses a Boost That said, the impact on financial markets is difficult to quantify. The most visible effect is on financial stocks, whereas the healthcare sector has not responded to the political storm over Obamacare.

Linkages Between the United States and Rest of World Are Entrenched The US stock market's strong showing in 2017 was influenced by better-than-expected growth abroad and a weaker dollar that caused earnings to reaccelerate. The bottom line is that whether we like it or not, the US economy and markets increasingly are influenced by global developments, and attempts to move toward protectionism would prompt a market backlash.

Investors Should Be Prepared for Increased Market Volatility The odds of repeating what happened in 2017 are low, and it is only a matter of time before volatility spikes. The risk is a stock market correction of 10–20%, rather than a prolonged bear market (Note: This occurred in Feb 2018).

Investors Should Also Factor in Longer-Term Challenges in Setting Their Strategic Asset Allocations Problems posed by an aging population, a steadily expanding entitlement system and widening income disparities are not top of mind now, but they are vital to our economy and political system over the long term.

Noteworthy Developments in 2017

Following Donald Trump's surprise election victory, I was asked about the implications for financial markets, and whether it would be a game-changer for the economy and markets. While it was soon evident investors were drawn to

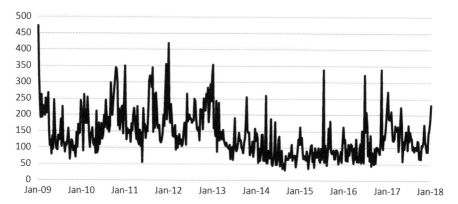

Fig. 10.1 Economic policy uncertainty index. (Source: Economic Policy Uncertainty)

Trump's pro-growth, pro-business agenda, they also faced challenges in positioning portfolios.

One of the biggest was to decipher what Trump would do as President. Indeed, he had no prior political background, lacked a coherent political philosophy and was prone to tweet frequently and make off-the-cuff statements that the media feasted upon. My advice to investors was twofold. First, I urged people to be as objective as possible and not to base their investment decisions on their political views, which are often emotional. Second, I stressed the importance of focusing on news that would impact the economy and financial markets, especially legislation that would be enacted, while ignoring the noise emanating from politicians, the media and the internet. The high degree of uncertainty following the election outcome is illustrated in Fig. 10.1, which provides a measure of economic policy uncertainty.[1]

Another major challenge was the political campaign revealed few details about forthcoming legislation. The clearest articulation of tax policy was the House bill drafted by Speaker Paul Ryan and Kevin Brady, Chair of the House Ways and Means Committee, in the summer of 2016. While it offered a starting point to analyze prospective changes in the tax code, it was unclear at the time whether Congressional Republicans who favored tax reform would call the shots or President Trump, who favored large tax cuts. My advice for investors was to stay flexible, as the process of reaching agreement would take considerable time, and tax legislation might not be enacted until 2018.

In the meantime, investors had to grapple with several political surprises. One of the biggest—gridlock was not dead. This became evident in the numerous attempts to repeal and replace Obamacare, and in subsequent feuds between the President and Republican leaders in Congress. These developments increased uncertainty about whether other key pieces of legislation in

---

[1] See Scott R. Baker, Nicholas Bloom and Steven J. Davis, Centre for Economic Performance, CEP Discussion Paper No 1379, October 2015.

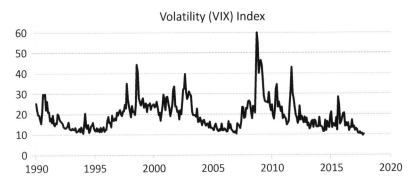

Fig. 10.2 Stock market volatility falls to all-time lows. (Source: CBOE)

the Republican agenda would be enacted. Further adding to uncertainty were heightened tensions with North Korea and differences over issues relating to trade and climate change between the Trump administration and US allies.

Yet, throughout 2017 financial markets remained remarkably unaffected by these developments. Equities, high-yield bonds and other risk assets posted outsized returns, while US stock market volatility was the lowest in decades (Fig. 10.2). This, in turn, raised questions about why markets were so calm, how long the calm would last and how investors should position portfolios for such an unusual environment.

As 2017 unfolded it became increasingly evident that investors maintained laser-focused on the US economy and prospects for US businesses. The key factor propelling stocks and other risk assets higher was a recovery in US corporate profits after five consecutive quarters of decline. This turnaround owed much to developments outside the United States, as prospects for the euro-zone, Japan, China and emerging economies improved. They bolstered oil prices following a steep decline, and together with a softer dollar they contributed to improved earnings for US multinationals and exporters.

Looking ahead, the key issues investors need to consider include the following: First, can the US economy break out a 2% growth trap? Second, if so, will business capital spending follow suit and help boost productivity growth, which is key to sustaining higher growth? Third, how will prospective policies impact taxes, the federal budget and interest rates? Fourth, how real are the threats of trade conflict and protectionism?

Favorable Near-Term Prospects

In the second chapter of this book, we examined reasons why the US recovery following the 2008 financial crisis has been more muted than previous recoveries. Unlike the 1930s, when John Maynard Keynes provided a new paradigm to explain the worst depression in history, there is no consensus today about

Table 10.1 Global economic growth, 2016–2019 in percentage (Consensus forecasts 2018–2019)

	2016	2017(e)	2018(f)	2019(f)
World	3.2	3.6	3.7	3.7
G-10	1.7	2.2	2.1	1.8
United States	1.5	2.3	2.5	2.1
Euro area	1.8	2.3	1.9	1.6
Japan	1.0	1.5	1.3	0.9
EM	4.3	4.7	4.9	4.9
China	6.7	6.8	6.4	6.2
India	7.1	6.4	7.5	7.4

Source: IMF, Morgan Stanley

Note: Figures for 2017–2019 are consensus forecasts

why US economic growth has been subpar for a decade. The chapter presented four explanations for the slowdown that emphasize different factors.

Of the four, the most commonly held view is that the GFC was caused by excessive credit creation, and the private sector—households and businesses—needed to reduce debt outstanding to more sustainable levels. Research by Reinhardt and Reinhardt suggests that it typically takes many years—on average about a decade—to bring household and corporate debt back in line with the trend in GDP.[2]

The good news is the latest crisis is unfolding in a similar manner, as US households and businesses have worked their way through most of the debt overhang, and housing prices have recovered considerably from their lows. As 2018 was underway confidence readings for consumers and businesses were at elevated levels, and surveys of small businesses indicated they were prepared to continue adding to jobs and to add to capital spending. And even though the unemployment rate was nearing 4.0%, wage and price pressures remained moderate. Consequently, market participants were anticipating the Federal Reserve would proceed cautiously in raising short-term interest rates.

While other advanced economies have lagged the US expansion, their economies accelerated in 2017 (Table 10.1). Both the eurozone and Japan were experiencing their best growth since 2010, and their economies appeared to be on a growth trajectory of 1.5–2.0%, with businesses posting solid earnings growth. In China, efforts by the government to maintain economic growth of at least 6% were also bearing fruit, although concerns about a bubble in the property sector persisted. With the advanced economies having achieved a synchronized expansion, prospects for emerging economies were also being upgraded as prices for oil and other commodities firmed.

At the beginning of 2018 forecasters were revising their US growth projections upward to the vicinity of 2.5% or higher. The main reason was the tax bill

[2] Reinhardt and Reinhardt, op. cit.

enacted at the end of 2017 provided tax cuts that were front-end loaded: Estimates of the stimulus provided in 2018 ranged from 1.0% to 1.3% of GDP. The tax cuts were expected to boost both consumer spending and business capital spending in the 2018–2019 time frame, as reflected in elevated levels for both consumer and business confidence.

OBSTACLES TO REVIVING LONG-TERM GROWTH

While the worst of the financial crisis is over and cyclical forces point to an upturn, most economists nonetheless do not expect the US economy to revert to its former trend growth rate of 3% per annum because of powerful secular forces at play. First, growth of the labor force has slowed to about 0.6% from an average of 1.2% in prior decades, and it is expected to decelerate further as immigration stalls. Second, growth of labor productivity has also slowed by more than a full percentage point over the past two decades.

There is a wide range of views among prominent economists about the prospects for improving productivity growth. Robert Gordon does not hold out hope for a quick reversal, mainly because the recent productivity trend is in line with the long-term average, and growth in labor supply is unlikely to increase. Larry Summers and other economists who subscribe to the "secular stagnation" thesis believe increased investment is the key to restoring long-term growth, but they also argue that interest rates will have to remain negative after inflation to bring this about. Finally, John Taylor and other market-oriented economists are more optimistic, although they believe it will require less government interference in the economy and more predictable monetary and fiscal policies. Robert Barro of Harvard is among the most optimistic, as he estimates the tax bill could boost long-term growth by 0.3% per annum.[3]

The main body of the book discussed a diverse array of policies that affect prospects for the overall economy and key sectors such as healthcare, financial services and international trade. In assessing these policies, it is useful to categorize them as to whether they primarily influence the demand side of the economy and have a short-term impact, or whether they are geared to the supply side, which shapes long-term growth.

During the worst of the GFC in 2008 and the first half of 2009, policymakers sought to counter declines in household and business spending, deleveraging of balance sheets and heightened demand for liquidity. The Bush administration lobbied Congress to pass the TARP program, where the proceeds eventually were used to recapitalize financial institutions, and the Obama administration followed with an $800 billion stimulus package. Meanwhile, the Federal Reserve lowered short-term interest rates to zero, and pursued quantitative easing to inject liquidity into the financial system.

These programs succeeded in stabilizing financial markets by the spring of 2009, and the economy began to recover by the middle of the year. Although

---

[3] See Barro, op. cit.

the pace of economic growth was well below the average for other recoveries in the post-war era, the unemployment rate fell steadily in ensuing years, as the Fed continued its program of purchasing financial assets to encourage greater risk taking by investors.

As the recovery spread, economists debated the desirability of pursuing fiscal and monetary stimulus in the wake of a ballooning federal budget deficit that reached 10% of GDP in 2009, and concerns that the Fed's unorthodox policies were distorting capital markets. Keynesian-oriented economists such as Larry Summers and Paul Krugman favored large, permanent increases in government spending to bolster aggregate demand, as well as low or negative real interest rates to spur business investment. However, as the problem lingered for nearly a decade, many economists questioned whether demand-oriented policies would be effective in promoting long-term growth. Market-oriented economists such as John Taylor, Glen Hubbard and Larry Lindsay argue that these policies added to investor uncertainty and thereby inhibited economic growth.

Return to Supply-Side Policies

Following the 2016 elections, the Trump administration and Republican-controlled Congress were decidedly in favor of policies to spur growth of the private sector by altering the tax code for businesses and households and by reducing regulatory burdens that businesses face. Market participants reacted favorably to this pro-business stance, viewing it as a return to supply-side policies of the Reagan era. However, there are several key differences between conditions then and today that investors need to consider.

The most significant difference is that inflation and interest rates were at very high levels in the early 1980s, whereas they are near record lows in the current environment. One of the main factors that contributed to the resurgence of growth in the 1980s was the Federal Reserve's commitment to rein in inflation and inflation expectations, which paved the way for sustained declines in US interest rates. Today, by comparison, the Fed is beginning to normalize monetary policy by raising short-term interest rates and scaling back its balance sheet very gradually. Thus, what had been a tailwind for the economy could become a headwind if inflation were to resume. The appointment of Jerome Powell as Fed chairman and four new governors also raises the question of whether the Fed will pursue its former policies or alter them.

A second key difference is that personal tax rates and the unemployment rate are much lower today than they were when President Reagan assumed office. Consequently, the stimulus to the economy from cuts in personal taxes is likely to be smaller. The case for corporate tax rate cuts is more compelling, because the United States has one of the highest corporate rates among advanced economies, and it has encouraged US businesses to shift production abroad and to retain profits there.

A critical issue for investors to weigh is whether lower corporate taxes will be effective in boosting subpar capital spending. The latter has been an important reason for the slow pace of the expansion and for diminished productivity growth since the GFC. It is also the principal argument the Republican establishment has used to garner support for a tax bill. However, as noted in Chap. 5, there have not been enough changes in the tax code to draw a strong conclusion about the likely impact on business investment. Also, businesses have been less willing to increase capital spending over the past two decades, primarily because they have earned above-average returns by hiring inexpensive workers while economizing on capital spending. Thus, record low interest rates have had relatively little impact in spurring investment activity, and the same may be true if corporate tax rates are lowered.

Whatever the impact on the economy, the prospect of corporate tax cuts has been an important factor supporting the stock market. Also, the combination of lower tax rates and less burdensome regulations has had a significant effect in boosting the confidence of many smaller businesses. This segment of the economy is typically the main engine for job growth during economic expansions. Because it is difficult to quantify the overall impact of deregulation, it is difficult to assess the impact on financial markets. Nonetheless, the effects are real and they contributed to a rally in small cap stocks.

Looming Budget Deficits and US Monetary Policy

Corporate tax cuts and deregulation are definitely positives for equity investors, but the potential for outsized budget deficits is a negative for the bond market. One of the main critiques of the tax legislation is that it will add to the federal budget deficit when federal debt outstanding already is at a high level of 77% of GDP and the unemployment rate is near a record low. While the original proposal submitted by the House GOP leadership in the summer of 2016 was deficit neutral, a compromise package was worked out with the White House and Senate leadership in which federal debt outstanding was targeted to rise by $1 trillion over the coming decade.

The rise in bond yields thus far is not concerning considering how low they are and how gradual the rise has been. However, the budgetary situation is likely to deteriorate in the next few years as more baby boomers retire and add to burdens on the healthcare system. While equity investors are focused on the magnitude and composition of corporate tax cuts, bondholders care about how the tax cuts will be financed. If they are additive to the federal deficit and debt outstanding, they could cause real interest rates to rise, which could adversely impact the stock market at some point.

For its part, the Federal Reserve under the new chair, Jerome Powell, is prepared to continue raising interest rates slowly as the economy gains momentum, while shrinking its balance sheet incrementally. At its final meeting in 2017, Fed policymakers signaled that three quarter-point rate hikes could be in the offing in 2018, which would match the increases in the prior year. The bond market, however, was pricing in only two rate hikes, mainly because core inflation remained comfortably below the Fed's 2% rate target, and wage increases had stayed moderate. Nonetheless, the risk is that wage increases and inflation will accelerate as the labor market continues to tighten, although it is difficult to pinpoint when this will occur. Despite the rate hikes and asset sales, the conduct of monetary policy has been highly accommodative, as judged by various indices of financial market conditions. They included relatively unchanged long-term bond yields, narrower corporate credit spreads versus treasuries, a buoyant stock market and a softer dollar.

THE DOG THAT DIDN'T BARK: TRADE WARS

While risks assets were supported by the prospect of tax cuts and deregulation in 2017, market participants were also relieved that President Trump did not follow through on his campaign threat to impose across-the-board duties on China, Mexico and other countries. Early on, the President recognized that China could play an important role in pressuring the government of North Korea to negotiate a settlement over nuclear weapons with the United States, and he backed off from imposing trade sanctions. He also agreed to renegotiate the NAFTA treaty with Mexico and Canada, rather than abrogating it. Meanwhile, there were ongoing negotiations with various countries to reduce the bilateral US trade imbalances that included discussions of areas in which US businesses claimed they received unfair treatment.

Still, there is a distinct possibility the President will pursue a more aggressive stance on trade issues, especially if he believes trading partners are not cooperating. Indeed, one area in which the President has been remarkably consistent over several decades is his view that bilateral US trade deficits are a sign of weakness. During the first quarter of 2018, the White House boosted tariffs on aluminum, steel, solar panels and washing machines, and also on Chinese imports of $50 billion. These actions fueled concerns about a possible trade war and resulted in heightened market volatility. Moreover, some observers are concerned the President could decide to allow NAFTA and the Korea–US trade agreement to lapse, which could unsettle financial markets further.

One of the messages of this book, however, is that trade imbalances are the result of macro forces that influence saving-investment decisions both at home and abroad. During the 1980s and early 1990s, the most important factor contributing to enlarged US trade deficits was the expansion in US budget deficits. Beginning with the turn of the century, however, enlarged US trade deficits increasingly were associated with rising surpluses in China and other Asian economies, which acquired massive holdings of US dollar-denominated reserves. It was also during the decade of the 2000s that job losses in manufacturing became more prevalent. Accordingly, there are valid reasons for the US government to take a tougher stance with China and other Asian countries to limit the size of their trade surpluses and their holdings of foreign exchange reserves.

That said, the US government must also be cognizant that threats to impose trade sanctions would inevitably invite retaliation. If so, it could result in a decline in the volume of world trade that would be very harmful to the world economy. Indeed, one of the important lessons from the market developments during 2017 is the crucial role that international economies played in boosting global growth and corporate profitability.

How Long Will Markets Stay Calm?

This issue became increasingly prevalent in 2017, as the stock market experienced one of the longest stretches of gains in history without even a minor pullback. It was especially surprising considering the political mayhem in Washington, DC, and heightened tensions with North Korea at the time.

The prevailing view among investors throughout 2017 was that risks of recession or inflation were both low, and the Federal Reserve would proceed very gradually in normalizing monetary policy. With interest rates at low levels, the strategy many investors pursued was to grab yield wherever they could find it, while underweighting bonds relative to stocks. Indeed, this strategy has been the key to outperforming markets since the economy stabilized from the GFC in the first half of 2009 (Table 10.2).

Looking ahead, the relevant issue is whether investors should continue to bank on the trend being their friend, or begin to position portfolios defensively. We have had ongoing debates about this issue at my firm, Fort Washington Investment Advisors. Our conclusion is that it is prudent to pare back holdings of risks assets when valuations become stretched, but as 2018 began we did not believe it was the time to shift portfolios into safe assets such as treasuries and cash. The main reason was the near-term economic outlook was positive.

There was a possibility the US economy could have a breakout year, in which real GDP growth approached the 3% threshold for the first time since the 2008 financial crisis. That said, we made some tactical changes such as lightening holdings of high-yield bonds when credit spreads versus treasuries have narrowed below historic norms.

Table 10.2 Returns for asset classes, pre- and post-global financial crisis

	Sept 30, 2007–Mar 8, 2009	Mar 9, 2009–Dec 31, 2007
S&P500	−41.4%	19.2%
Russell 2000	−43.0%	19.8%
EAFE ($)	−45.2%	13.2%
MSCI EM ($)	−45.3%	13.3%
US Treasury	10.4%	2.5%
IG credit	−2.1%	6.8%
High yield	−20.1%	13.1%

Source: S&P500, Russell, Morgan Stanley, U.S. Treasury, Barclays, Merrill Lynch

The more formidable issue is how to view the valuation of the stock market. Using traditional P/E ratios, the market appears expensive relative to long-term norms. However, as Jeremy Grantham has pointed out, the average ratio for the past 20 years is considerably above that for the pre-1997 period. Furthermore, this shift coincides with a jump in US corporate profits as a percent of GDP, as well as with a decline in real bond yields.[4] At the start of 2018, equity strategists were revising upward their projections for 2018 earnings in the wake of the tax legislation, with the consensus calling for profit growth in the low double digits. Therefore, it is not obvious that the stock market is grossly mispriced, despite its remarkable run since March 2009. Accordingly, our firm has been neutral on the market since mid-2015, after having overweighted it beginning in the first half of 2009.

At the beginning of 2018, I felt that the stock market was overdue for a correction. Therefore, I was cautious about increasing exposure to US equities at the time. But I did not favor large-scale reductions in equity holdings, because the likelihood of an asset bubble appeared low. Typically, they occur when there is rapid credit expansion, the property sector becomes frothy and financial institutions are overexposed to the sector.[5] But those conditions have not been evident for the past decade. Also, despite the market's huge run-up since 2009, investor sentiment did not appear euphoric. According to Cornerstone Macro, for example, many investors are cognizant that the investment cycle is in its later stages, and they have been gravitating to defensive plays such as large cap stocks with franchise value rather than more speculative small cap names.[6]

Concluding Thoughts: Reflections on Three Mega Trends

The typical investment horizon for institutional investors is the short-to-medium term: Three to six months for fixed-income portfolio managers and nine months to a year for equity managers. However, for most individuals it is prudent to have a longer-term horizon in mind—a decade or more —to determine their strategic asset allocations, whether conservative, balanced or growth oriented. Therefore, people need to be cognizant of secular trends that have influenced returns for the various asset classes in the past, and the prospect they could change in the decade ahead.

Specifically, three mega trends should be considered: (i) Will inflation stay low throughout the coming decade? (ii) How will demographic shifts in the United States and rest of world impact saving rates, the budget and real interest rates? (iii) Will globalization continue to be a dominant force, and if so will it exacerbate the problem of widening income disparities?

---

[4] Grantham, op. cit., pp. 10–11.
[5] See Sargen, op. cit., for a discussion of asset bubbles.
[6] See Francois Trahan and Stephen Gregory, Cornerstone Macro, "The Year in Stock Selection: 2017 Scorecard," December 27, 2017.

The most important trend influencing returns on financial assets since the early 1980s has been a steady reduction in inflation and inflation expectations. It has directly bolstered returns on fixed-income investments as bond yields have fallen on a trend for the past 35 years. While many investors thought yields were poised to rise at the turn of the millennium, the surprise was they continued their descent in the wake of the GFC, which created deflationary pressures. By now, most investors have thrown in the towel, believing inflation and interest rates will stay low for the foreseeable future. While this outcome is possible, one needs to recognize we live in unchartered waters with central banks having kept interest rates unusually low for a decade now. There is no precedent to know what could cause inflation to accelerate in these circumstances. However, as the unemployment rate approaches 4%, there are early indications of nascent wage pressures that should be monitored.

A second long-term trend is the aging of the US population and the impact it is having on the federal budget and on pension funds. When Medicare and Medicaid were launched in the 1960s, the US population was considerably younger than today and lifespans were shorter. In the meantime, however, the burden of entitlement programs on the federal budget has become increasingly evident. Politicians are wary about altering these programs to make them actuarially sound for fear of a backlash by the electorate. Yet, as discussed in Chap. 3, we may only be 10–15 years away from the day when entitlement programs (including Social Security and interest on the national debt) take up all federal revenues and discretionary spending must be financed out of increased debt issuance. Clearly, this trend is not sustainable and it remains to be seen when politicians will act to alter it.

The third trend to consider is globalization. In the book we have argued that it was a leading force contributing to global growth in the 1980s and 1990s, but it has become more controversial in the past two decades, as China and other emerging economies compete with the United States and other advanced economies in the production of manufactured goods. This has led to a backlash in which nationalism and populism have emerged as political forces in the United States and Europe. While many of the criticisms ignore the positive effects on economic growth and business profitability, there is no denying it has exacerbated the division between well-educated, affluent people and those who lack the educational requirements to compete in the global market place. Our political leaders therefore must recognize the importance of improving educational attainment for the populace as a whole, as well as to realize there is no quick and easy fix for this problem. Failure to deal with this problem, after all, would have significant adverse consequences for our economy and political system.

Finally, one of the central messages of this book is that the United States faces important policy choices ahead. While politicians typically focus on issues that influence the outcomes of elections, the policies that will have the greatest influence on the economy's long-term potential are ones that will take years to play out. They entail undertaking reforms of the tax code, the healthcare system, the educational system and the regulatory system to improve the economy's productive potential. With the US economy fully recovered from the 2008 crisis, now is the time to begin to address these issues.

Index[1]

[1] Note: Page numbers followed by 'n' refer to notes.